...munities
...and Infor...
...u...

Calderdal...
...in...
...ed

C000180343

...DUE F...

BULGARIA

POCKET GUIDE

Discover the world's best destinations with the Insight Guides Walking Eye app, available to download for free in the App Store and Google Play.

The container app provides easy access to fantastic free content on events and activities taking place in your current location or chosen destination, with the possibility of booking, as well as the regularly-updated Insight Guides travel blog: Inspire Me. In addition, you can purchase curated, premium destination guides through the app, which feature local highlights, hotel, bar, restaurant and shopping listings, an A to Z of practical information and more. Or purchase and download Insight Guides eBooks straight to your device.

TOP 10 ATTRACTIONS

ALEXANDER NEVSKI CATHEDRAL
The pride of Bulgaria's capital Sofia, with glittering domes and a fascinating crypt. See page 35.

VELIKO TARNOVO
One of the country's most picturesque cities. See page 63.

BACHKOVO MONASTERY
A haven of fine religious art and architecture. See page 58.

SANDSTONE PYRAMIDS
These structures stand guard near Melnik. See page 48.

BANSKO
The ski resort has much to offer besides the pleasures of the piste. See page 49.

RILA MONASTERY
A holy site set among the mountains and adorned with gorgeous frescoes. See page 50.

THE NATIONAL HISTORY MUSEUM
Bulgaria's treasure house. See page 37.

ISKAR GORGE
Follow its long and spectacular course. See page 41.

NESSEBUR
The jewel of Bulgaria's Black Sea coast, Nessebur has an excellent beach and a medieval Old Town. See page 79.

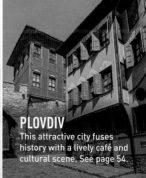

PLOVDIV
This attractive city fuses history with a lively café and cultural scene. See page 54.

A PERFECT DAY

9.00am

Breakfast
Head for the Radisson, whose enormous breakfast buffet – in summer held on the terrace – is open to all comers and offers the only breakfast in town with views towards the Alexander Nevski Cathedral.

10.00am

A trinity of churches
The heart and soul of Sofia, the Alexander Nevski never looks better than at mid-morning, sunlight reflecting off its domes. Take in nearby Sveta Sofia and Russian Churches too.

12 noon

Museums
Check out the two museums which share the Tsar's former palace on Boulevard Tsar Osvoboditel: the Ethnographical Museum and the National Art Gallery.

11.30am

Souvenirs
The streets around the Nevski cathedral are home to a wide variety of stalls and street hawkers. Look out for naïve art, lace and embroidery. At weekends a flea market sells all sorts of enjoyable junk.

1.30pm

Halite lunch
Head inside the Halite – Sofia's 19th-century market hall – and join local people lunching on great-value food from the stalls on the lower ground floor, which incorporates Serdica ruins. You can also find local produce ranging from meat and fish to cheese and sweets.

IN SOFIA

3.00pm

Ancient and modern Sofia
Take a look at the icons inside the Sveta Nedelya church before heading over to TZUM for a whizz round the trendy new stores. The Sheraton Hotel Balkan's smart bar is a great place for an expensive pit-stop.

10.00pm

On the town
Sofia stays up late. Choose a spot in one of the many cafés and bars around the National Theatre on Alexander Battenberg Square and settle in for a long night.

2.15pm

The Rotunda
Sofia's oldest building houses some amazingly well-preserved 10th-century frescoes and is surrounded by Roman ruins ripe for exploration.

5.00pm

Street life
Remind yourself that this is a truly Balkan city – where life happens on the street – by promenading the city's busiest and most famous avenues, Vitosha and Graf Ignatiev.

7.30pm

Dinner
Take yourself to Sofia's best restaurant – Secret. The work of one of Bulgaria's best-loved chefs, Secret serves contemporary twists on Bulgarian classic dishes in a luxury setting.

CONTENTS

INTRODUCTION

Long ago, Bulgaria was the most powerful country in Europe. That is a title it no longer has, but it can still lay claim to being one of the most fascinating. It is certainly different. A place where east meets west, it is perhaps fitting that this was one of the few places on earth where, for 40 years, East Germans could meet their West German relatives with ease. All this at a time when Bulgaria was the staunchest ally of the Soviet Union, upholding an orthodox socialist regime, yet also, during the 1960s, the first Soviet ally to develop its massive potential as a tourist destination.

Since Bulgaria peacefully waved goodbye to Communism in 1990, tourist facilities have become even better. From the beach resorts and fishing villages of the Black Sea to the ski centre of Bansko; from the provincial-in-size yet cosmopolitan-in-attitude capital of Sofia to the historical region around Veliko Tarnovo, Bulgaria still offers tremendous value for money, while preserving its uniqueness.

Bulgaria's eight million people are slowly coming to terms with their place in contemporary Europe. In the 1990s many Bulgarians voted with their feet, emigrating en masse to Spain and Italy in particular. However, now that Bulgaria is an EU member, with a resilient economy and a stable political climate, the country is no longer losing its people at such an alarming rate. Indeed, many of those who left a decade ago are returning.

Nevertheless, in foreign eyes it will be some time before the image of Bulgaria as a Balkan backwater is eroded. But the country has never been backwards, rather a dynamic mix of rural and urban, ancient and modern, traditional and innovative. Whereas in other Balkan countries cultural diversity has had the potential to be destructive, in Bulgaria it has always been celebrated.

THE COUNTRY AND ITS CLIMATE

Bordered by Romania to the north, Serbia and Macedonia to the west, Greece and Turkey to the south and a deceptively short coastline of 378km (235 miles) along the Black Sea to the east, the Republic of Bulgaria covers some 110,993 sq km (42,855 sq miles), an area about the size of Ireland. The capital, Sofia, where a fifth of the population lives, lies in the west of the country, at the apex of the two great mountain ranges that sweep through the country: the Balkans range, which extends almost to the Black Sea, and the Rila/Rhodopes range, which runs south into Greece and east into Macedonia. The highest mountain in the country is Mt Moussala, at 2,925m (9,596ft) the tallest in the entire Balkan Peninsula.

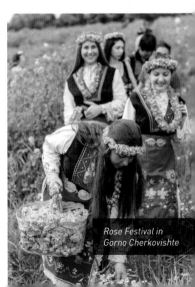

Bulgaria suffers from climatic extremes, with winters usually bitterly cold, and summers, especially along the Danube plain, often extremely hot. Average temperatures in Sofia in January range from 4–2°C (25–36°F), while in August they usually climb to over 30°C (86°F). Precipitation levels

Rose Festival in Gorno Cherkovishte

throughout the year are high. Outside the dry Danube plain, you never have to wait long for a downpour in Bulgaria.

POPULATION AND LANGUAGE

More than 85 percent of the population speaks the official language, Bulgarian. Another 2.5 percent speaks Macedonian, considered in the country to be a Bulgarian dialect and not a separate language. Bulgarian is written in the Cyrillic alphabet – the traveller would do well to learn the characters – created in the 9th century by followers of two Salonika-based Bulgarian monks, Cyril and Methodius (see pages 18 and 122). So proud are Bulgarians of the alphabet that they have even given it a national holiday (May 24, Education Day). Other minority languages include Turkish – spoken by 9 percent of the population – and the related languages of Gagauz, Tatar and Albanian. Small pockets of Romanian speakers (Vlachs) also exist along the eastern Danube.

The name Bulgaria – land of the Bulgars – is something of a misnomer. Today's Bulgarians are descendants of a number of peoples: the Slavs, Greeks and Macedonians, as well as the Bulgars. Much as the Angles gave their name to England without ever being the most populous group in the country, so the Bulgars were just one of many peoples who formed the Bulgarian state. They were the most astute politically, however, playing one tribe off against another, and they quickly became the ruling

Making a gesture

Bulgarians nod their heads when they mean 'no' and shake their heads when they mean 'yes'. Don't be caught out. Ask a kiosk vendor if she has any bus tickets, and a shake of the head means 'as many as you like'. It is easy to get confused.

class after arriving in the Balkans from an area now known as Old Bulgaria, situated between the Black and Caspian seas.

RELIGION AND CULTURE

The majority of the population – around 90 percent – is Bulgarian Orthodox. There is a significant Catholic minority, while western Protestantism, in the form of the Baptist and Methodist churches, has become increasingly popular since 1990, and is the country's fastest growing faith. Most of Bulgaria's Turks remain Muslims, although over 250,000 left Bulgaria in the summer of 1989 – mainly for Turkey – during the 'Great Exodus'.

Bachkovo Monastery

It is perhaps the Bulgarian Orthodox Church that has most strongly influenced Bulgarian culture. But what is specifically Bulgarian and what is merely Balkan? So much culture is shared between the countries of the region (language, music, folklore, even food) that while the Bulgarians are clearly a different people to the Serbs, for example, it is difficult to gauge what makes them so. Yet there are specific cultural achievements of which Bulgaria is proud. The Thracians, who emerged in the 2nd millennium BC, were unsurpassed in the exploitation of metals: the best examples are to be found in the Pangyurishte treasure. Then there are the frescoes of the Boyana church, 13th-century masterpieces that anticipated the Renaissance. This points to a cultural

Hiking in the Pirin Mountains

heritage that has withstood a turbulent history.

LANDSCAPE AND WILDLIFE

Bulgaria is blessed with natural wonders. The beaches of the Black Sea are among the finest in Europe. The interior is marked by the great mountain ranges, with plains in between. Visitors who come at the end of April can enjoy skiing one day and sunbathing the next.

Yet while skiing is popular, mountain hiking remains the preferred pastime and Bulgarians see walking up the nearest mountain as something of a rite of passage. Even during the winter it is not uncommon to see courting couples wandering up or down a piste. The best hiking is offered by the Pirin Mountains, the most spectacular of the Bulgarian ranges, while the Rhodopes offer less demanding hikes. Lovers of lakes head for the Rila range.

Bulgaria's mountains and lowlands are also rich in wildlife, and offer excellent opportunities for birdwatchers. The marshlands around Bourgas (known as the Strandzha) and the Madzharovo nature reserve in the Rhodopes are the best birdwatching areas. Bears are still sometimes seen in parts of the Rila and Rhodope mountains.

Bulgaria has three national parks: Pirin, Central Balkan and Rila, as well as nine nature reserves, of which two, Pirin and Sreburna, are on Unesco's World Heritage list.

A BRIEF HISTORY

History in the Balkans is often less the study of past events and more an examination of national pride, with a good deal of myth and legend thrown in for good measure. Though Bulgaria's history is not exceptional, the simple fact that the Cyrillic alphabet was invented by followers of two Bulgarian monks has ensured that the modern Bulgarian story has been well documented for far longer than that of most other nations in the region.

THRACIANS, ROME AND BYZANTIUM

While there are traces of ancient settlements in Stara Zagora, the history of Bulgaria really begins with the emergence of the Thracians on the Danubian plain around 1200 BC. The Thracians were an amalgamation of earlier tribes, who may have migrated to the region from Mesopotamia. Archaeological evidence suggests that there was certainly communication between the Near East and the Balkans across the Black Sea by the end of the 2nd millennium BC.

The first documented history of the region comes from the Greeks, who began to visit Thrace in the 7th and 6th centuries BC, gradually extending their influence from the coast inland. Though Persian invasion briefly disrupted this Hellenisation in the 6th century BC, Philip of

> ### Valley of Kings
>
> In 2004 a number of archaeological discoveries were made south of the Stara Planina Mountains in an area dubbed the 'Valley of the Thracian Kings'. The findings include a 2,400-year-old Thracian shrine near Shipka, believed to be the burial chamber of King Seuthes III, rival to Alexander the Great.

Macedonia conquered Thrace in 346 BC and began colonising the area, building settlements, including one that carried his name, Philopopolis, the present-day Plovdiv. Under Philip's son, Alexander the Great, the Thracian interior was fully opened up to Greek settlers and merchants, who over the next 200 years fused with the Thracians to form a distinct ethnic group.

Rome conquered Thrace in AD 46 and wasted no time in colonising the area. The region prospered. New towns were settled, including Serdica (Sofia), Augusta Traiana (Stara Zagora) and Durostorum (Silistra). But the Roman Empire became overstretched and in AD 260 Dacia (present-day Romania, to the north) was abandoned to Barbarians. Thrace, too, came under constant Barbarian attack. The Roman Empire was split between Rome and Constantinople (Byzantium) in 395, but it was not until the reign of Emperor Justinian I (the Great, 527–65) that imperial authority was once again imposed over all of present-day Bulgaria.

THE SLAVS

Though Justinian encouraged culture and education, fortified the cities of the border lands and quickly settled Serdica and Philipopolis with great numbers of people, the continued power vacuum in Dacia to the north meant that Thrace remained susceptible to invasion. Barbaric, ill-organised tribes such as the Pechenegs and Avars did not get far, but in the 5th century the Slavs, a much larger tribe, swept into the Balkans. Their origins are unclear, though they migrated into the Balkans from a region thought to be in Poland and Ukraine, and are the forefathers of present-day Croats, Czechs, Serbs, Slovaks, Slovenes, Poles and Russians, as well as Bulgarians. So immovable were these Slavs that they were not opposed by the Byzantine rulers, who allowed them to settle.

THE FIRST BULGARIAN KINGDOM

No sooner had the Slavs gained hegemony over Thrace than a new wave of immigrants arrived, this time the Bulgars. Politically astute and brilliant horsemen, the Bulgars were described more than once in Byzantine dispatches as 'barbaric and vulgar'. Originating in a region east of the Black Sea, perhaps as far as the Caspian Sea, the Bulgars followed the Black Sea shore, entering Thrace by the Danube Delta. As many as 250,000 came and, led by Khan Asparuh, they established in 681 the Parvo Bulgarsko Tsarstvo (the First Bulgarian Kingdom). Its capital was Pliska.

The next 200 years are the most fiercely debated in Bulgaria's history. While many Bulgarian historians insist that the tolerance of the Slavs and the enlightened rule of the Bulgars meant that the two nations fused effortlessly – with the Slavs eventually accepting Bulgar dominance – most Western historians see things differently. They claim that only political expediency – the Bulgars needed Slav support – held the uneasy alliance together.

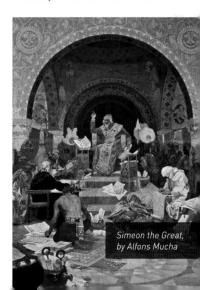

Simeon the Great, by Alfons Mucha

SIMEON THE GREAT

Of all Bulgarian leaders, one remains more revered than any other: Simeon the Great (reigned 893–927). During his reign, Bulgaria conquered huge swathes of Europe and became the largest empire on the continent, stretching from Greece to Ukraine, from the Black Sea to the Adriatic. Simeon, who had been schooled in Constantinople and knew the value of a good education, used the newly created Cyrillic alphabet as a means of uniting Slavs. More than a warrior, Simeon was a man who realised the importance of culture in uniting a nation, and his patronage of the arts gave birth to the first real age of Bulgarian literature, painting and sculpture.

Yet Simeon greatly overstretched his resources and on his death left no heir capable of replacing him. The Bulgarian empire collapsed, the country once again falling under the spell of Constantinople.

THE SECOND KINGDOM

Byzantium, however, was by this stage an empire in disarray, and it was not long before the Bulgarians regrouped and reclaimed their country; albeit somewhat reduced in size

⊘ THE CYRILLIC ALPHABET

Although the alphabet only took one man's name, Cyrillic is the work of two monks: Konstantin-Cyril and his brother Methodius. In 855 the two brothers retired to a monastery in Salonika (in modern Greece) to formulate a satisfactory way of rendering the scriptures into the Slavic language. Seven years later they emerged with a rune-based script known as the Glagolitic alphabet, which one of their former pupils helped adapt to create a prototype of today's Cyrillic alphabets. This in turn was finessed by the various Slavic peoples to fit local nuances. Cyrillic is used today in Bulgaria, Serbia, Macedonia, Russia, Belarus, Ukraine, Mongolia, Turkmenistan, Tajikistan and Kyrgystan (see page 122).

Cyril and Methodius, fathers
of the Glagolitic script

from its days under Simeon. Two brothers, Peter and Assen,
led a Bulgar uprising at Mizia, and declared a new Bulgarian
Kingdom, with its capital at Veliko Tarnovo.

Assen's son, Tsar Kaloyan, further extended Bulgaria,
recapturing Varna in 1204, the year the knights of the Fourth
Crusade sacked Constantinople and declared their Holy
Eastern Empire. Kaloyan was unimpressed and shortly afterwards defeated the Crusaders and set about creating an
empire of his own. He was murdered in a palace coup and
replaced by Tsar Boril, briefly, before the far more satisfactory
Tsar Assen II took power in 1218. Expansion recommenced and
Bulgaria was again – briefly – the size it was under Simeon.

OTTOMAN DOMINATION AND THE NATIONAL REVIVAL

The defeat of the Serbs by the Ottoman Turks at Kosovo
Polje (Blackbird Field, in Kosovo) in 1389 sealed the fate of

Bulgarian freedom fighter statue at Dryanovo Monastery

the Balkan Peninsula. In 1393, Veliko Tarnovo was captured by the Turks, and three years later all of Bulgaria became part of the Ottoman Empire. This period of Turkish rule, which lasted nearly 500 years, came to be called the Ottoman Yoke.

The list of atrocities committed by the Turks during the Yoke is a long one. At least half the Bulgarian population was killed or left to starve in the first 50 years following the conquest, while many of those who survived were forced to convert to Islam – though a good number resisted. Arabic replaced Bulgarian as the official language used at court, and Greek became the language of the church.

The occasional uprisings against the Turks, including those at Veliko Tarnovo in 1598 and 1686, never succeeded in bringing about anything resembling change. It was the dominance of Greek priests, appointed by the Turks to oversee the Bulgarian church, which forced a number of Bulgarian intellectuals to take measures to ensure that the Bulgarian language and a Bulgarian-centred history survived. Many intellectuals, such as Bogdan Bakshev, Archbishop of Sofia, were forced to publish their works outside of Bulgaria. Bakshev's *History of Bulgaria* caused a furore when published in the 17th century, as did Pasii of Hilender's *History of the Slav-Bulgarians* (1762). Both works helped rekindle Bulgarian nationalism in the 19th century – a period known as the National Revival. Economics also played a part in the Revival, as an increasing number of wealthy Bulgarians were able to travel to trade in areas not dominated by Turkey, and in doing so returned with new liberal ideas that were anathema to Bulgaria's rulers.

THE STRUGGLE FOR INDEPENDENCE

In 1859, with Russian help, Romania rid itself of the Turks. Ten years later the Bulgarian Revolutionary Committee (BRCK) was created in Bucharest, uniting disparate nationalists for the first time under one group behind one leader, Vasil Levski. The capture and execution of Levski in 1873 provided the movement with a martyr, and in April 1876 it was ready to launch an uprising against the Turks.

During the April Rising, more than 30,000 rebels died, evoking great sympathy from Russia and the Western powers, which until then had urged Turkey to grant Bulgaria autonomy, not independence. Russia declared war on Turkey in 1877 and, after a year of heavy fighting, the Ottoman Empire was forced to sign the humiliating San Stefano Peace Treaty. On 3 March 1878, Bulgaria declared independence.

THE THIRD BULGARIAN KINGDOM

The other great powers – Britain, France and Austria-Hungary – were not happy with the treaty, and the Congress of Berlin in July of 1878 reversed much of the San Stefano Treaty. Macedonia was returned to Turkey in its entirety, while the rest of the country was divided, creating two provinces that had to pay annual tributes to the Sultan of Turkey, while remaining nominally independent.

Searching Europe for a monarch, the Bulgarian assembly chose Alexander Battenberg to serve as prince, who repaid them by creating an autocratic state in which he wielded

Boris III in 1920

considerable power. He is remembered favourably, however, for managing to reunite the divided country (in 1885) against the will of Britain and France. He was replaced as prince on his death in 1887 by Ferdinand Saxe-Coburg, who changed his title from prince to tsar in 1908. Bulgaria then proclaimed full independence from Turkey, and with the Ottoman Empire in chaos, nobody objected.

THE BALKAN WARS AND THE DIFFICULT 1920S

Bulgaria united with Serbia and Greece in an alliance designed to rid the Balkans of the Turks forever. The First Balkan War of 1912 saw them achieve that goal, almost capturing Istanbul in the process. Then the victors fought between themselves over the spoils in 1913, Bulgaria suffering defeat at the hands of erstwhile allies Serbia and Greece. As a result Macedonia was lost to Serbia, and the Dobruja was lost to Romania.

World War I saw the vast majority of the population side with Russia and its allies, while the government – a sworn enemy of Serbia, Russia's ally – backed the Axis powers. The result was carnage, and defeat in September 1918, after which deserting soldiers attempted a coup, which failed, though it did force Ferdinand to abdicate in favour of his son, Boris III.

Macedonian nationalists of the Internal Macedonian Revolutionary Organisation (IMRO) were a thorn in Bulgaria's side throughout the early 1920s. Opposed to the newly created Yugoslavia, the IMRO was hostile to the policies of Prime Minister Alexander Stamboliski, who sought peaceful co-existence with Yugoslavia. In alliance with military officers, the IMRO staged a coup in 1923, killing Stamboliski and creating a shaky coalition that managed to hang on to power, with Boris III still nominally the head of state, until 1935. In November of that year, Boris decided he had had enough of politicians and dismissed the lot, creating an absolute monarchy.

WORLD WAR II

Bulgaria sided with Germany for a second time in 1941, though the country remained to all intents and purposes neutral, refusing to send troops to the Russian front despite German protestations. There was a German military presence in the country throughout the war, however, and as the tide turned and the Red Army swept through the Balkans, Bulgaria was quick to see which way the wind was blowing, changing sides on 9 September 1944, a date until recently celebrated as Liberation Day.

COMMUNISM

With the Red Army in control of the country, it was impossible for Bulgaria to avoid a post-war Communist takeover. Bulgarian Communists who had fled to Moscow in the 1920s and had survived

Thompson village

A tiny village in the Iskar Gorge is named after Major Frank Thompson, sent to Bulgaria to evaluate the fighting potential of the local partisans during World War II. Thompson, a committed Marxist, quickly went native and was killed fighting alongside the partisans in 1944. After the war he was revered by the Bulgarian Communist regime as an anti-fascist hero.

Stalin's purges now returned, led by Georgi Dimitrov, who had been leader of the Comintern in the 1930s. Elected in a mockery of an election in 1946, Dimitrov immediately had a Communist Party-dominated parliament rubber stamp a new constitution (based on that of the Soviet Union), which abolished the monarchy and created the People's Republic of Bulgaria.

Dimitrov died in 1949 and was replaced by Valko Chervenkov, who eradicated all actual or potential opponents, most of whom perished in the death camps of Belene, on the Danube. Chervenkov fell out of favour with Moscow after Stalin's death in 1953 and was replaced by Todor Zhivkov, who remained absolute ruler until 1989. Zhivkov's rule is marked by economic stagnation and utter subservience to the Soviet Union.

RETURN TO DEMOCRACY

Eastern Europe's year of revolutions and political change, 1989, appeared to have passed Bulgaria by and, as late as November, Zhivkov's grip on power appeared as tight as ever. He was undone, however, by reformers inside the Communist Party, who forced him to resign, arresting him on charges of fraud. The reformers, who had overseen small but significant changes in the economy from the mid-1980s onwards, elected Peter Mladenov as head of the Central Committee, promising multiparty elections for June 1990. Since then Bulgaria has struggled with the transition to a market economy, but remained relatively politically stable. Simeon Saxe-Coburg, who was king briefly in the 1940s, oversaw Bulgaria's entry to Nato, but failed to deal with rampant corruption. He was replaced in 2005 as prime minister by Sergei Stanishev, a left-winger, who secured Bulgaria's entry to the EU in 2007. Since 2009, the centre-right former mayor of Sofia, Boyko Borisov, has dominated Bulgarian politics, and is currently serving his fourth spell as prime minister.

HISTORICAL LANDMARKS

c.1200 BC Emergence of Thrace as an organised state.

356 Philip of Macedonia conquers Thrace.

681 First Bulgarian Kingdom.

855–62 Cyril and Methodius lay foundations for the Cyrillic alphabet.

865 Christianity adopted as state religion.

927 The Bulgarian Empire reaches its zenith under Simeon the Great.

1018 Emperor Basil II conquers Bulgaria and makes it part of Byzantium.

1185 Second Bulgarian Kingdom created.

1396 Bulgaria becomes part of the Ottoman Empire.

1491 Rila Monastery decorated.

1732 Rozhen Monastery rebuilt.

1876 April Uprising by nationalists put down by Turkey.

1877 Russo-Turkish Wars of Liberation.

1878 Bulgaria declares independence from Turkey.

1879 Sofia becomes capital of Bulgaria.

1912–13 Balkan Wars: Bulgaria, Serbia and Greece unite to defeat the Turkish Empire before fighting each other over the spoils.

1914 Bulgaria sides with the Axis powers in World War I.

1923 Military coup overthrows left-leaning government.

1935 Tsar Boris III declares an absolute monarchy.

1941 Bulgaria enters World War II on the side of Germany.

1944 Soviet Union conquers Bulgaria. Communists take power in 1946.

1953 Todor Zhivkov becomes leader of Bulgaria.

1955 Bulgaria is a founding member of the Warsaw Pact and Comecon.

1978 Bulgarian agents kill émigré dissident Georgi Markov on Waterloo Bridge in London by stabbing him with a poisoned umbrella.

1989 More than 250,000 Turks flee to Turkey; Zhivkov dismissed.

1990 Reformed Communists win general elections.

2004 Bulgaria joins Nato.

2007 Bulgaria joins the EU on 1 January.

2010 Bulgarian Irina Bokova becomes first woman to head Unesco.

2017 Boyko Borisov becomes prime minister for the fourth time.

Stefan Stambolov Street in Veliko Tarnovo

WHERE TO GO

The best of Bulgaria comprises the capital, Sofia, and the Rila and Pirin mountains to the south; the historically significant Balkan range that sweeps through the centre of the country; and the Black Sea coast. Using the country's three largest cities of Sofia, Plovdiv and Varna, as well as the smaller but regionally important Veliko Tarnovo, as bases – all with excellent hotel, restaurants and services – most of the country can be explored quite easily. And wherever you go, you are seldom far from a sight of historical or natural significance.

SOFIA

Overlooked from the south by the 2,290m (7,515ft) high Cerni Vrah, **Sofia** ❶ nestles snugly at an altitude of just under 600m (1,970ft). Home to just under one and a half million people, almost a fifth of the country's total population, it has a history going back to the Roman settlement of Serdica, but almost all of its important buildings and monuments, like the modern state they help define, are less than 150 years old. Visitors arriving either by road from the airport or by train will be disappointed at their first impressions of the Bulgarian capital. Sofia requires a little perseverance from the

Street names

Some useful terms to know when navigating the streets of Bulgaria's cities, towns and villages are: *bulevard (bul)* – boulevard or avenue; *ploshtad (pl)* – square; and *ulitsa (ul)* – street. You'll find that churches are usually named after a saint: *sveti/sveta (sv)*.

visitor, for once through the encirclement of monolithic, dilapidated Soviet-era apartment blocks, the city centre is a gem.

Most sights are contained within the area bordered by boulevards Evlogi Georgiev, Hristo Botev, Slivnitsa and Vasil Levski. This area can be divided into three different (though not distinct) districts: **Imperial Sofia**, centred on the Nevski Cathedral, St Sofia and the Yellow Brick Road, **Byzantine and Ottoman Sofia**, around Sveta Nedelya, the Sheraton Hotel and Banya Bashi Mosque, and **Modern Sofia**, the city's commercial hub along boulevards Vitosha and Graf Ignatiev.

MODERN SOFIA

Modern central Sofia, which stretches from the inner ring road to ploshtad Sveta Nedelya (St Nedelya Square), is by no means

The magnificently ugly NDK

an architectural wonder. The most modern building is the magnificently ugly **National Palace of Culture**, known by locals and marked on most maps as the NDK. Built in 1981 as a multi-purpose cultural venue, it stands guard at the southern entrance to the city centre – it cannot be missed – without a single redeeming feature.

The area in front of the NDK is known as **pl Bulgaria**, or **Yuzhen Park**. It has some decent summer terraces, and often plays host to outdoor events, including rock and pop concerts. Though the fountains are attractive (when they are working), the square is dominated by the enormous, eye-catching (for all the wrong reasons) **1,300 Years of Bulgaria Monument**. This folly was conceived in the early 1980s when the Bulgarian Communist Party was reinventing itself as a more nationalist movement. Links with Bulgaria's glorious past, however tenuous, were encouraged. It commemorates the anniversary of the founding of the 'first unitary Bulgarian state' in 681, after Khan Asparuh defeated a Byzantine army at the Danube Delta.

Straight ahead you will find **Vitosha Boulevard**, Sofia's main shopping street. Vitosha has long been a centre of commerce, and the street is pleasant enough on the eye, with most of the post-World War II buildings being no taller than four or five storeys. Shops, cafés, street traders and surprisingly wide pavements make a stroll along Vitosha a pleasant experience.

Stray dogs

Bulgaria has a large stray dog population. Though the dogs rarely bite, they often bark at passers by, attacking occasionally. It is to be hoped that the authorities will soon rid the country of this problem (in some cities, including Sofia and Plovdiv, they by and large have). Should you be bitten, go to the nearest hospital for a series of rabies injections immediately.

At the northern end of Vitosha is the city's only pedestrian street, **Pirotska**. Lined with cafés and shops, it is worth exploring for bargains. Running parallel to Pirotska is Ekzarh Yosif, where you will find Sofia's **synagogue Ⓐ**, the largest in the Balkans. Built between 1903–09 the synagogue (Mon–Fri 9am–4pm, Sat 10am–2pm except Passover) can accommodate 1,200 worshippers. Today, however, most services are held in the smaller rooms at the front, as Sofia's Jewish population has dwindled to below 5,000 from around 50,000 before World War II.

At the far end of Pirotska is the city's largest market, **Zhenski Pazar**, or women's market (daily sunrise–sunset). Selling mainly produce, the market also has clothes, craft and bric-a-brac stalls selling good souvenirs, though you may

Sofia's synagogue

have to hunt through a large amount of tat to find something worthwhile. The real charm of the market is just watching the locals shop.

A better place to look for bargains is **Graf Ignatiev Boulevard**, which runs at a 45-degree angle from Vitosha to the river. Close to the southern end of Graf Ignatiev is the decrepit-looking **Sv Sedmotchislenitsi Church** (7am–7pm, services daily 8am and 5pm), dedicated to Sts Cyril and Methodius, the

Bulgarian brothers who created the Cyrillic alphabet (see pages 18 and 122). Although less than impressive from the outside, the church's interior is exceptional, with well-preserved frescoes.

BYZANTINE AND OTTOMAN SOFIA

At its northern end, Vitosha Boulevard leads into **pl Sv Nedelya** **Ⓑ**, the traditional heart of the city, dominated today by the Sofia Hotel Balkan, though there is much more to its charms than that splendid building alone.

The centrepiece of the square is the church that shares its name, **Sv Nedelya** (7am–7pm, services daily 8.30am and 5.30pm), which stands on what was the very centre of ancient Serdica. This 19th-century building is the latest in a long line of churches on the site. The outside is not impressive, but the inquisitive visitor is rewarded on entering by some of the finest icons and most colourful murals in the country. On leaving, note the plaque that commemorates (in Bulgarian) the fact that assassins attempted to kill Tsar Boris III here by planting a bomb in the church during a service in 1925.

The **Grand Hotel Balkan**, behind and to the right of Sv Nedelya, is part of a much larger building; the rear is occupied by the **Presidency** (entry only by appointment), the offices of Bulgaria's president. The two guards who ceremoniously stand erect at the modern glass entrance are an anachronism in their *ancien regime* costumes, but a picture-postcard sight nonetheless.

Directly next to the hotel is TZUM, once the state-run department store selling little of any interest to anyone, today a modern, multi-level shopping centre playing host to a wealth of big brand name stores. Across the road is the ghastly **Statue of Sofia**, put up in haste on a whim of the mayor in 2001. To the right of TZUM in the centre of a small park is Sofia's only surviving, working mosque, the **Banya Bashi**. On the other side of the same square, behind graffiti-strewn hoardings, are the majestic **Municipal Baths**, first built in 1913 in a style which pays homage to Bulgaria's Byzantine connections, and which today host the **Sofia History Museum** (Tue–Sun 10am–6pm). The museum tells the story of the city from ancient times to the 1940s by way of eight excellent exhibitions.

Directly opposite the baths is the **Halite** (daily 6am–8pm), the century-old central food market, which sells all kinds of local food, from meat and fish to cheese and sweets. The lower level has been expertly adapted to incorporate Serdica ruins, where local people make use of a number of food outlets at lunchtime.

Past the entrance to the Presidency is a large court-yard which hides the city's oldest building, the **Sv Georgi Rotunda** (Mon–Sun 8am–5pm; donations expected). Built for an unknown purpose in the 4th century, it became a church in the 6th century and is today surrounded by part of Sofia's visible **Roman ruins**. Much of what you see on the outside of the rotunda, however, is relatively new, and major restoration work was not always carried out with as much care as it could have been. The Roman ruins look similarly out of context surrounded by red brick. The real glory of the rotunda lies in its interior: three layers of original frescoes can still be seen, the oldest dating back to the 10th century.

Opposite the Presidency is the **Archaeological Museum** Ⓒ (Apr–Oct daily 10am–6pm, Nov–Mar Tue–Sun 10am–5.30pm), which is housed in the former Grand Mosque, built in 1494. Many of Bulgaria's finest treasures from Thracian, Roman and Byzantine times (including two enormous Roman sarcophagi) are displayed here. The golden burial masks and medieval icons are particularly worth seeking out. The monumental building on the other side of the road is the former Communist Party **Central Committee Building**, from where Bulgaria was

ЗАВЕДЕНИЯ ЗА БЪРЗО ХРАНЕНЕ

ТЪРГОВСКА ГАЛЕРИЯ

The Halite food market

run for the best part of 50 years. The building was topped by an enormous red star during the Communist era, and a rather limp flag today tries hard to fill the breach.

Moving further along, the **Largo**, or **Yellow Brick Road** (because of the now rather faded yellow cobbles), occupied mainly by foreign embassies and government offices, leads to the **Tsar's Former Palace**, today the Ethnographical Museum and National Art Gallery, on the right, opposite the **Alexander Battenberg Square**. Until 1999, the centrepiece of the square was the stark mausoleum of Georgi Dimitrov, the first Communist leader of Bulgaria who died in 1949. Dimitrov's remains were removed in 1990, and the building itself demolished nine years later. The southern end of the square has a host of good cafés and restaurants, almost all of which have tables on terraces during the summer, while the outdoor café in front of Bulgaria's **National Theatre** on the eastern side is one of the best, trendiest and most expensive places to drink coffee in the city.

Walking back to the Tsar's Former Palace at the northern end of the square, the two museums now housed inside are worth visiting, depending on what's on. The **National Art Gallery** (Tue–Sun 10am–6pm) has no permanent exhibition, and changing exhibitions highlight the works of the country's leading artists, for which guided tours are available in English, with notice, during the week.

Far more interesting is the **Ethnographical Museum** (Tue–Sun 10am–6pm), where the collection includes a good selection of Bulgarian traditional clothes and costumes, arts, crafts and musical instruments. Children in particular will love it. The small gift shop sells good-value souvenirs.

Sv Nikolai Church

Turning left out of the palace, the next building on the left is **Sv Nikolai (Russian) Church D**. Built quickly over the winter of 1912–13 on the whim of a Russian diplomat, it is the loveliest church in the city, as its relatively small size prevents it from being overwhelmed by the ostentation that smothers many other churches. The onion domes that give away its heritage were repainted in gold leaf donated by Mother Russia. The church's most interesting facet is the **crypt** (daily 7.30am–6pm), which houses the body of Bishop Serafin, a popular local religious leader who died in 1950, and who was too revered by the local population to be buried in the anonymous grave the recently installed Communist regime wanted.

IMPERIAL SOFIA

The Third Kingdom of Bulgaria did not last long. Yet from independence from Turkey in 1878 to the exile of King Simeon II in 1946, regal Bulgaria embarked on a campaign of building and modernising its capital that was at once breathtaking in its speed and impressive in its lasting grandeur.

Of all Sofia's wonders the **Alexander Nevski Cathedral** ❸ (daily 7am–7pm, services daily 8am and 5pm, Sun Mass 9.30am), which stands in a square of the same name, remains the most enduring. Its immaculate golden domes, restored to their original splendour with gold leaf donated by the Russian Orthodox Church, still dominate the city's skyline and glitter in any amount of sunlight; even a dull day can be brightened by their sparkle. Built between 1882 and 1912 in the elaborate neo-Byzantine style of the time, the cathedral is named after St Alexander Nevski, the Russian tsar who led his country to victory over Sweden in 1240. He was the patron saint of Tsar Alexander II, the Russian monarch at the time of the cathedral's construction.

The **Alexander Nevski Crypt** ❻ (Tue–Sun 10am–6pm), entered down the stairs on the left-hand side of the church's main doors, is the best museum in Sofia and possibly the top attraction in the country. The collection of Old Bulgarian art on show is outstanding, and there are few museums offering a better selection of iconography anywhere in the world. Highlights include the altar doors from the Pogonovo Monastery, dating from 1620, as well as the doors from the

Orlitso Nunnery at the Rila Monastery, paintings executed in 1719. All exhibits have captions in Bulgarian and English, and there is an excellent shop selling fine replicas and other Bulgarian souvenirs.

In front of the cathedral is Sofia's oldest church, the **Sv Sofia** (daily 9am–6pm), which gave the capital its name. Built in the 5th century on the highest point in the city, the church has been destroyed and rebuilt a number of times. The Turks used it as a mosque from the 16th century onwards. The present building dates from the late 19th century, built to replace the previous structure (which had a minaret), which was destroyed in Sofia's last great earthquake in 1858.

The area between Sv Sofia and the cathedral is dominated by a small but infinitely interesting **flea market**, the perfect place to buy Todor Zhivkov portraits, Orders of Lenin medals and Hermann Goering fountain pens.

⊘ VASIL LEVSKI

On his execution in 1873, the Bulgarian revolutionary Vasil Levski became a martyr for the Bulgarian independence movement; today he is remembered as the country's greatest revolutionary and his name adorns streets, stadiums, monuments and sports teams. Born in 1837, Levski became a professional revolutionary in his early 20s, and quickly became the symbolic leader of the Bulgarian nationalists, travelling in secret around the country to raise funds and find recruits. He was betrayed by Dimitar Obshti, who, when arrested in December 1872, told the Turks all he knew about the Bulgarian revolutionary movement. Levski was arrested and hanged in Sofia the following February; the spot is marked by the Levski Monument.

Opposite the cathedral is the **Bulgarian Parliament** building, while behind is the **National Library**, with **Sofia University** next to that on the other side of ul 19 fevruari. The strange statue at the northern end is in fact the much heralded **Vasil Levski Monument**. This peculiar erection marks the spot where Levski was hanged in 1873 by the Turks for allegedly planning an anti-Ottoman revolt.

The city's oldest church and namesake, Sv Sofia

SOFIA'S OUTSKIRTS

Sofia offers a number of delights away from the bustle of the centre, in the hills that lead up towards Vitosha National Park. The most important, and an essential stop on a trip to Bulgaria, is **Boyana Church G** (Tue–Sun 9.30am–5.30pm; additional charge for tours in English and other languages) in the suburb of Boyana, a 20-minute taxi ride (around 12 leva) from the city centre. Listed by Unesco as a World Heritage Cultural Site, Boyana was built over two centuries from around 1050 to 1259, when the frescoes for which it is famed were executed. More than 250 people are depicted on the walls in a style that anticipates the Renaissance. The painter's identity is unknown.

Armed with a good map you can make your way on foot in about 20 minutes from Boyana to the splendid **National History Museum H** (Apr–Oct daily 9.30am–6pm, Nov–Mar 9am–5.30pm).

Walk back from Boyana to the Daskal Sv Popandreev and follow bul Pushkin to where it meets ul Radev. The huge building on the right-hand side, well hidden behind a tall fence and enormous garden complex, is the Boyana residence, former home of the Communist Party boss **Todor Zhivkov**. The entrance to the museum, housed in a smaller building, is easily found by taking ul Gabrovnitsa, the first turning on the right as you pass the residence. If you don't fancy the downhill walk, you won't have to wait long for a taxi at Boyana, as visitors come and go all the time. You can also take the infrequent bus No. 63 from church to museum.

The National History Museum was relocated to its current Boyana setting in 2000. The move caused a scandal at the time, but the judgement of the city's authorities has proved to be sound. The museum's former home in the Palace of Justice in the centre of town was cramped and dark, whereas the present location allows the stunning collection of well over 22,000 exhibits to breathe. The museum is well laid out, and many of the best exhibits have English captions, though maps showing the Bulgarian Empire's rise and fall are captioned in Bulgarian only. Familiarity with the Cyrillic alphabet (see page 122) would help here. Highlights include jewellery dating from 500 BC, the Pangyurishte treasure – 6kg (13lb) of gold commissioned by Thracian King Seuthes III – and much early Christian ico-nography. Children will enjoy the small play area in the rear of the museum, as well as the MIG fighter jets that are on display at the front.

Getting back to the centre of Sofia from the museum is easy: take trolley bus No. 2 from its terminus at the car dealer-ship directly opposite the museum to pl Makedonia.

☉ TODOR ZHIVKOV

Bulgaria's former Stalinist leader Todor Zhivkov cut a sorry figure in the 1990s, one far removed from the hated dictator who had terrorised a country for nearly 40 years. Zhivkov assumed leadership of the Bulgarian Communist Party in 1954, having outmanoeuvred his rivals following the death of Georgi Dimitrov in 1949. Zhivkov's leadership was characterised by slavish loyalty to the Soviet Union, often at the expense of Bulgaria's own interests.

Of all Zhivkov's disastrous policies, which contributed to the utter bankruptcy of the economy, it was his treatment of Bulgaria's Turkish population that secured him a place in the pantheon of the most despised Communist leaders. During the 1970s and 1980s Turks were persecuted merci-lessly by Zhivkov's regime until, in the summer of 1989, hundreds of thousands voted with their feet and headed for Turkey.

Arrested in November 1989 immediately after the re-gime changed hands, a mockery of a trial in 1990 found Zhivkov guilty of embezzlement and, though he was sen-tenced to life imprisonment, he spent the years until his death in 1998 under comfortable house arrest.

VITOSHA

The presence of the Vitosha Mountains just 10km (6 miles) from the centre of the city makes Sofia one of the most fortunate capitals in Europe. Access to **Vitosha National Park** from Sofia is easy: a taxi will cost no more than 10 leva to either the **Dragalevtsi chair lift** or **Simeonovo gondola** stations. Public transport to both is surprisingly unreliable outside the ski season (December to April).

Dragalevtsi a charming village offering a number of good places to stay and eat, is most famous for its **monastery ❶**, built in the mid-14th century. Though little of the monastery remains, the original 14th-century church and a few of the original cloisters – one of which sheltered revolutionary Vasil Levski from the Ottoman secret police in the 1860s – are in good condition, while the gladed setting alone is well worth the 15-minute walk up from the chairlift station. **Simeonovo** is a less interesting village, notable only for its access to Vitosha via its gondola, which is quicker than the Dragalevtsi chairlift, and during winter queues here are shorter.

Both the Dragalevtsi and Simeonovo lifts terminate at **Aleko**, the heart of Vitosha, at an altitude of 2,000m (6,560ft). From here a small number of chair and drag lifts radiate out to form a half-decent ski area in winter, though advanced skiers will be bored in a day or two as there are few difficult pistes around Aleko. The hotels up here all rent out ski equipment and can arrange for instruction. Aleko is swamped by Sofians every winter weekend, so it's best to ski from Monday to Friday. The spring, summer and autumn are different stories entirely. The chairlifts usually operate only at weekends, but with locals usually preferring to walk the well-marked paths, you should never have to wait too long. The tallest peak in the range, **Cerni Vrah** at 2,290m (7,515ft), can be scaled by the fit in an hour's hike from Aleko.

The striking Iskar Gorge

DAY TRIPS FROM SOFIA

There are several worthwhile attractions in the vicinity of Sofia, but they are scattered to all points of the compass at varying distances from the city. The best solution if you wish to explore the area is to stay in the capital and hire a car, perhaps combining two or three destinations in a day if they are in the same general direction.

NORTH OF SOFIA

There are several routes leading north from the capital. The most striking follows the 156km (97-mile) **Iskar Gorge ②**. Narrow and bumpy in places, it is rarely busy, and there are plenty of places to pull over along the way to admire the views. The most stunning parts of the gorge are between **Novi Iskar** and **Lyutibrod**, an area that was almost completely cut off from the rest of Bulgaria until the railway was built in the 1890s. The road came much later. Even today the only settlement of any size is **Svoge**, situated in one of the remotest and most spectacular parts of the gorge, where the Iskar and Iskrets rivers meet.

The mountains north of Sofia have the greatest concentration of **monasteries** in the country. The most accessible is the **Cherepish Monastery ❸**, which is located close to where the Iskar Gorge peters out around Lyutibrad. Legend has it that in the 14th century Tsar Ivan Shishman fought and defeated an unnamed enemy here – probably the Turks – before beheading the dead and burying their skulls on the site where the monastery was built shortly afterwards. Locals insist that the very name of the monastery (*cherep* means 'scalp' in Bulgarian) attests to

⊙ HRISTO BOTEV

The poet Hristo Botev, the most romantic of all Bulgaria's revolutionaries, was born in Kalofer, near Kazanlak, in 1848 – Europe's year of revolutions. Exiled to Romania in 1867, after provoking the wrath of the Turkish authorities with his nationalist public speaking, Botev threw himself into literary pursuits, acting as an editor of a number of émigré newspapers, as well as writing increasingly nationalistic poetry. He became de facto leader of the Bulgarian Revolutionary Committee in 1873 after Vasil Levski's execution, and presided from afar over the disastrous April Revolt of 1876. After the revolt had been crushed, Botev, with 200 supporters, attempted to galvanise Bulgaria's nationalists in support of a new revolt, only to be killed on 20 May by a Turkish patrol while making his way to the town of Vratsa. His 1875 volume, *Songs and Poems*, remains the finest work of Bulgarian national poetry.

the truth of the myth. Today, the monastery is known more for its 15th-century gospel bound with gold covers and the Festival of the Assumption on 15 August, when it is swamped by day-trippers from Sofia.

Cherepish Monastery

More off the beaten track is the **Sedemte Prestola Monastery**, which lies nestled in wooded hills about 15km (9 miles) along the side valley of the Gabrovnitsa stream (turn off the main gorge route at Eliseina). Built in the 11th century, destroyed and rebuilt in the 18th, the monastery was always a popular refuge for outlaws, bandits and nationalists.

Further north is the small town of **Vratsa**, gateway to **Vratsa Gorge ❹**, which begins just 2km (1.2 miles) beyond the city centre and is an excellent day-trip on its own. There are two good museums to visit, the **Ethnographical Museum** and the **History Museum** (both Tue–Fri 9am–5.30pm, Sat–Sun 9am–noon and 2–5pm). The Ethnographical Museum has a number of Revival-period houses, and a large warehouse displaying 19th-century Orazov horse-drawn carriages. The History Museum's highlight is the peerless **Rogozen treasure**, a stash of silver found in 1985 in nearby Rogozen village, dating from the 5th century BC.

The only other town of note further north is **Berkovitsa**, once famous for its pottery but now a ski resort, although a small **Ethnographic Museum** does try to keep the city's heritage alive.

Kukeri dancer, Pernik

EAST OF SOFIA

Known to all Bulgarian schoolchildren as the cradle of the modern Bulgarian state, **Koprovshtitsa**, 75km (47 miles) east of Sofia, was the site of the ill-fated April Rising of 1876, when a rudimentary force of Bulgarian nationalists sought to spark a nationwide revolt that would finally free Bulgaria from the Turks. Though the rising was ruthlessly suppressed, it did at least raise international awareness of the brutality of the Turkish regime in Bulgaria, and the town has remained a symbol of Bulgarian nationalism and culture. For such reasons it is the host of a national music festival (held every five years, it is next due in August 2020). At an altitude of 1,060m (3,480ft), the town is also a popular mountain resort.

The primary attractions of Koprovshtitsa, however, are its **National Revival-period houses**, six of which are open to the public as museums (Apr–Oct Tue–Sun 9.30am–5.30pm, Nov–Mar Tue–Sun 9am–5pm). A ticket can be bought which is valid for entry to all six houses (with the exception of the Oslekov House). Guided tours of the houses in English are also available, although you should phone ahead to check.

WEST OF SOFIA

Pernik 5, 25km (15 miles) west of Sofia, is one of the best places in Bulgaria to witness the bizarre **Kukeri festivals** (see page 96) for which the country is famed. Over the last weekend of January thousands of men dress in costumes usually made of dead animals – including the heads – designed to evoke fear and scare off evil spirits. Dressed like this, they then spend long hours in a trance-like state dancing and chanting throughout the town. The origins of Kukeri are vague, but the practice is thought to have derived from the religions of the ancient Thracians.

Beyond Pernik, following the same road to Kyustendil, **Zemen Monastery** ❻ has Bulgaria's best collection of 14th-century frescoes, restored to greatness in the 1970s. The exterior of the monastery is not as lavish as others in Bulgaria and its position, on a hill hidden from the town of Zemen, is one of the most secluded. The meandering Struma river flows through the scenic 25km (15-mile) -long **Zemen Gorge**; however, the road skirts around the gorge so the only access is on foot (though the railway line does pass through it). The 70m (240ft) -high **Skakavitza waterfall** near the village of Kamenishka Skakavitza is just one of the highlights.

THE PIRIN AND RILA MOUNTAINS

Directly south of Sofia is the small Rila mountain range, known primarily for the Rila Monastery, Bulgaria's most famous attraction. Further south, stretching towards Greece, are the Pirin Mountains. Both ranges offer decent skiing (at Borovets in the Rila, at Bansko in the Pirin) and serve as good bases for hiking and walking, especially from the spa town of Sandanski.

BLAGOEVGRAD

The largest city in the southwest of the country, **Blagoevgrad** has a population of around 75,000 and sits at the foot of the Rila Mountains on the banks of the Blagoevgradaksa Bistritsa River.

A colourful pedestrian street in Blagoevgrad

A major spa resort since the 16th century, it has 30 hot springs, some with temperatures of up to 55°C (130°F). A centre of learning since the Rila monks set up a university in the 17th century, it today plays host to four universities and thousands of students who swell the population during term time. Though devoid of real attractions, apart from the fine **History Museum** (Mon–Fri 9am–noon, 1–5.30pm), Blagoevgrad is a worthy stopping-off point for its cultural mix and access to more interesting parts of the region.

With its annual influx of budding young minds, Blagoevgrad is one of the major cultural centres of Bulgaria. The city supports a chamber opera noted throughout the country, as well as the Pirin Folk Ensemble, Bulgaria's most popular folk music combo, which can be seen on stage at the American University when not on tour.

Out of town at Stob, a short bus journey from Blagoevgrad on the route to the Rila Monastery, are weirdly shaped natural red rock formations known as the **Stob pyramids ❼**. A well signposted path and set of steps from the main road makes access to the pyramids straightforward. The **Bachinovo Park**, just north of the town, is a favourite hiking venue, while further along the same valley is **Bodrost**, a spa resort and hiking centre that allows access to the **Parangalitsa** nature reserve and the ancient fortress of **Klissoura**.

SOUTH OF BLAGOEVGRAD

Close to the Greek border, **Sandanski** ❽ is another spa town, set in the Pirin foothills at an altitude of 240m (787ft). Named after Yane Sandanski, a Macedonian rebel who fought against the Turks, it is located on the site of an old Thracian settlement that made good use of the springs. The Romans built a huge public bath complex, the Askelpion, and the town flourished until the 6th century when it was destroyed and fell into decay. When Bulgaria was fully liberated from Turkey in 1912, the town had a population of around 500. Today it is home to 25,000. The town's large, if dated, **public bath complex** remains very popular and is well worth a day's bathing. Find it behind the cruise-ship-shaped Hotel Sandanski.

To the southeast of Sandanski is **Melnik** ❾, a living museum set gloriously amid steep slopes and crags. Once populated almost exclusively by Greeks, the town is now virtually deserted, never having recovered after being largely destroyed during the Balkan Wars of 1912–13. There remains, however, much to see. A number of Revival-period houses can be visited (opening times vary), while to the south of the town above the river, on the

Sandstone crags, Melnik

Nikolova Gora – about 30 minutes' walk uphill – are the **Sv Nikola Church** and the fearsome remains of a **Slav fortress**. The views of the town below are stunning.

Melnik is also the gateway to **Rozhen Monastery ❿**, which is 6km (4 miles) further on and accessible by bus. The original 13th-century monastery was burnt down; the current structure dates from the 17th century. Most visitors prefer to walk, however, either along the road or by two mountain routes – one taking about two hours, the other three hours; both are well signposted from Melnik. The road is popular because it passes some of Bulgaria's most spectacular **sandstone pyramids**, several more than 80m (260ft) tall, cut over thousands of years by the Melnik and Rozhen rivers, with rain doing the rest of the sculptural work. Most are not pyramids at all, but various odd-looking shapes.

Skiers in Bansko

BANSKO

The undisputed winter capital of Bulgaria, **Bansko ⓫** is the largest ski resort in the Balkans. Since the local council invested heavily in building a vast network of new ski lifts during the 2000s (including a gondola lift direct from the city centre to the ski area) this sleepy town – whose centre is packed with National Revival-era houses – has become one of the most popular skiing destinations in Europe. Although it shows some signs of over-development (the outskirts of the town are blighted by half-finished, abandoned or simply empty apartment complexes) the snow-sure skiing – almost all slopes are above 1,400m/4,600ft – a great selection of hotels and restaurants, and superb nightlife make Bansko an ideal choice for skiers and non-skiers alike.

There is far more to Bansko than skiing; the town has been a popular destination for many years. Its cobbled streets are lined with fine houses, many of which date from the beginning of the 19th century when the town was an important trading centre on the overland route from the Middle East to the Aegean Sea. Bansko grew rich on the back of commerce, and grand houses, churches, schools and cultural buildings sprang up apace. Although the town's prosperity suffered towards the end of the century, when the Danube was opened to traffic and the trade route ceased, Bansko was revived in the early 20th century as a weekend holiday destination for Sofians.

Even the planners of the socialist era preserved the atmosphere of Bansko, and the modern areas of the city around the central square, **pl Nikola Vaptsarov** – named after Nikola Vaptsarov, a revolutionary poet – blend with the old. The most notable sights in Bansko are centred on the older **pl Vazrazhdane**. The **Church of Sv Troitsa** is the largest in the region and was completed in 1835, when Bansko's prosperity was at its height. Large does not always translate as enthralling, however, and the outside of the church is rather bland. The interior is much more interesting, with icons painted by Dimitar Molerov, a leading figure in the Bansko School of Art that flourished at the same time as the town. The **stone tower** in the courtyard was added 30 years after the church had been completed.

Anyone with an interest in Bulgarian culture or history might like to visit the **Neofit Rilski House Museum** (Mon–Fri 9am–1pm, 2–5pm), located behind the church at ul Pirin 17. This was the childhood home of Neofit Rilski, a leading member in the Bulgarian cultural revival of the 19th century, who, among other achievements, was a member of the scholarly collective that first translated the New Testament into Bulgarian. The house has been preserved to retain its original appearance; inside photographs explain Rilski's career. The **Icon Museum** (Mon–Fri 9am–1pm, 2–5pm) in the **Rilski Convent**, on the other side of pl Vazrazhdane, is another gem, showcasing the works of Dimitar Molerov and his contemporaries, who produced countless masterpieces for the merchants of the town who patronised the Bansko School.

RILA MONASTERY

Northeast of Blagoevgrad lies the Rila range, and Bulgaria's most visited attraction. Rila Monastery. The Rila range is the sixth-highest in Europe and the Moussala, at 2,925m (9,600ft), is the highest mountain in the Balkans. The range is home to thousands of small lakes. Samokov is the region's main town.

Among the peaks, valleys, lakes and forests lies the world-famous **Rila Monastery** ⑫ (Apr–Oct daily 8.30am–7.30pm, Nov–Mar daily 8.30am–4.30pm), an outstanding example of National Revival-period architecture. It can be seen in a rushed day-trip from Sofia, but a more leisurely visit is recommended,

Church of the Virgin Birth, Rila Monastery

with tours departing from Borovets, Bansko and Blagoevgrad almost every day of the year. There is a regular bus service to the monastery from Blagoevgrad, Dupnitsa and the small village of Rila. Independent travellers with cars can drive to the monastery from Blagoevgrad in less than an hour.

A monastery has stood on this site since St John of Rila (Sveti Ivan Rilski, patron saint of Bulgaria) founded one in the 10th century, but the current structure dates from 1816–47, the original having been all but destroyed by the Turks in the 18th century. The East Wing Museum was completed in 1961.

From the outside the monastery looks like a medieval fortress, and the wonders of the interior are a hidden delight. The most spectacular of the monastery buildings is the **Church of the Virgin Birth**, with sublime porticos and colonnades. Inside the church, the elaborate icons and use of gold leaf betray the wealth of the monastery builders and the power that the

The Rafail Cross

A unique specimen of the art of woodcarving, the Rafail Cross in Rila Monastery is made from a piece of wood 81cm x 43cm (32in x 17in) in size. It was made in the latter half of the 18th century by a Rila monk, Rafail, who took 12 years to complete it. Interwoven in the miniature carving are 104 religious scenes and 650 small figures: the largest carving is no bigger than a grain of rice. Rafail used fine chisels, small knives and a magnifying glass in his work, and all but lost his sight as a result.

region once had. The **Hand of St John of Rila**, a relic of the saint, is kept inside the church, though it is rarely on display. Another treasure is the 12th-century **Icon of the Virgin**, which can usually only be seen on Assumption Day, 15 August.

The elegant **Tower of Hreylo** looms large beside the church, and is the only part of the original monastery that survives. The **Preobrazhenie Chapel** on the top floor houses a fine museum of 14th-century murals. Most of the original treasures of the monastery are now housed in the **East Wing Museum**, including the doors of the Hrelyo Church, icons and the beautiful **Rafail Cross** (see box).

Something resembling an entire village has now grown up around the monastery to serve the tourists and pilgrims who visit it all year round, including two hotels, the Tsarev Vruh and the Rilets, of which the latter is easily preferable. The monastery also offers the most basic of accommodation in its dormitories.

BOROVETS

The largest of Bulgaria's purpose-built ski resorts, **Borovets** has been playing host to visitors since the mayor of nearby Samokov built a chalet here for his wife in the 1890s to alleviate her tuberculosis; other wealthy families – including the tsar's – quickly followed suit. The resort remained an exclusive hideaway of the rich until the 1950s, when the Communist authorities developed it, primarily for the use of party members. The idea of investing heavily in hotels and ski lifts to attract foreign cash was a 1960s' afterthought. Since then the resort has seen massive development and is today dominated by two enormous hotels, the Rila and the Samokov, almost self-contained resorts in themselves. From the Rila a network of chairlifts and drag lifts branch out to form one of the ski areas, known as the **Sitnyakovo**, while a fast gondola lift takes skiers up to the second ski area, the **Yastrabets**, from its terminus just beside the Samokov. In all there are around 55km (35 miles) of piste in Borovets, some of it quite challenging. Snow is reliable from late December to the end of March.

Once the snow has gone, skiers give way to hikers, but this is not the best walking country in Bulgaria. The most interesting and, for the fit, challenging is the walk up to Yastrabets, which takes a good five hours, and from there onwards to the peak of Musala is another hour and a half.

Wherever you stay in Borovets, prices are usually cheaper as part of a package tour. Turning up

Borovets ski resort

on spec can be expensive, and at weekends during both the winter (February and March) and summer (July and August) high seasons is risky, as the resort can be full.

PLOVDIV AND THE RHODOPE MOUNTAINS

Plovdiv, in the Plain of Thrace, is the country's second-largest city, and perhaps the most picturesque. The Rhodopes, which spread out from the plain in a generally southerly direction, are a meandering range of mountains that offer good hiking and walking. There is skiing, too, at Chepelare and Pamporovo.

Philip of Macedonia founded **Plovdiv** ⑬ in 342 BC, and named the town Philipopolis after himself. For centuries it was little more than a garrison town, until the Romans developed

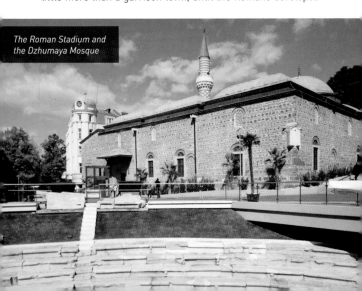

The Roman Stadium and the Dzhumaya Mosque

its potential as a trading halt on the route from Constantinople to Belgrade. Known to the Romans as Trimontium, Plovdiv today has a population of almost 400,000. It is a genuine rival to Sofia in terms of historical importance, and although a Sofian would baulk at the suggestion, given the variety of good hotels, cafés, bars and restaurants, its vibrant cultural scene and access to the Rhodopes, Plovdiv may indeed be a finer place to spend a few days than the capital itself.

DOWNTOWN PLOVDIV

The centre of modern Plovdiv is the megalithic **pl Tsentralen**, a public square too big for itself and the town, dominated by the Trimontium Princess Hotel, one of the city's best. Remains of the **Roman Forum** were discovered when the square was built, and are now preserved in an area next to the post office. The west of the square is bordered by the **Tsar Simeon Park**, a well-kept but attraction-free garden, popular with courting teenagers.

Leading directly northwards from pl Tsentralen is the pedestrianised **Alexander I Boulevard**, the major shopping street. The **Plovdiv City Art Gallery** (Mon–Fri 9am–5.30pm, Sat–Sun 10am–5.30pm) has a small, yet well curated, collection of both 19th-century and contemporary pieces. Look out for the seated statue of Milo: an eccentric who wandered the street for decades and became a symbol of modern Plovdiv.

At its northern end, bul Alexander I reaches **pl Dzhumaya**, a microcosm of Bulgarian history, containing the impressive ruins of a **Roman Stadium** and one of the most stunning mosques in the country, the **Dzhumaya Dzhamiya** (Sat–Thu). One of 53 mosques erected by the Turks in Plovdiv during their 500-year rule of the city, the Dzhamiya was built in the 14th century, during the reign of Murad II (1359–85). Its thick, high walls and 25m (82ft) -high minaret dominating the surrounding area. The area

The Roman Amphitheatre

of narrow streets behind the mosque is known as The Trap and has in recent years become a cultural and nightlife hub.

OLD TOWN

The best way to enter Plovdiv's **Old Town** is to follow ul Saborna, which meanders uphill to the Nebet Tepe Citadel from pl Dzhumaya. The first sight that looms on the right (up some steep steps) is the **Church of the Virgin Mary** (daily 7.30am–7pm) with a strikingly colourful pink and blue clock tower. A short detour from here is the splendid **Roman Amphitheatre.**

Built in the 2nd century during the reign of Emperor Marcus Aurelius, it is the best preserved Roman monument in Bulgaria. It is now used as a venue for operas, plays and concerts almost every evening throughout the summer, most notably the annual **Verdi Festival**, usually held during the first week of July. Back on ul Saborna you will pass the small **Gallery of Fine**

Arts (Mon–Sat 9am–5.30pm) and the **Apteka Hipokrat** (daily 10am–5pm), a fascinating – but again, small – pharmaceutical museum. Next comes the **House of Zlatyu Boyadzhiev** at No. 18 (Mon–Fri 9am–5pm), a gallery dedicated to Zlatyu Boyadzhiev, a talented modern painter whose reputation is tainted by his one-time willingness to please the Communist Party with socialist-realist works depicting idealised, happy peasants.

Two doors further along is the **Icon Museum** (daily 9am–12.30pm, 1.30–5pm) packed to the rafters with religious art from the surrounding region, while next door is the **Church of Ss Konstantin i Elena**, the oldest Christian church in Plovdiv, built on what was the wall of the original Macedonian fortress. Some of the icons inside date from the 14th century, although master iconographer Zahari Zograf added many more during the National Revival in the 19th century. Next to the church stands the **Hisar Kapiya**, the eastern gate of the Macedonian fortress, though little of the gate we see today is original.

From the gate, carry on up the ever steeper hill towards the shabby ruins of the **Nebet Tepe Citadel**. Plovdiv's stun-ning **Ethnographical Museum** (Tue–Thu, Sat–Sun 9am–noon, 2–5pm) is on the right, at ul Chomarov 2. Set in the large, charming former house of Greek merchant Argir Koyumdzhioglou, the museum collection is good, but it is the house (dating from the 1840s) and gardens that people come to see. Chamber concerts are performed in the gardens in the summer.

Passing back under the Hisar Kapiya, you reach the ornate **Museum of National Liberation** (Tue–Sun 9am–noon, 2–5pm) in the former home of a wealthy Turkish merchant. The museum is an excellent primer on the Bulgarian National Revival and struggle for liberation, with many exhibits carry-ing English captions.

SOUTH OF PLOVDIV – THE CENTRAL RHODOPES

Assenovgrad ⓮, the first town south of Plovdiv, is famed for its vineyards, but there is little here to keep you, apart from the medieval fortress, a short distance outside of town on the road to Smolyan, and the Bachkovo Monastery, second only to Rila among Bulgaria's finest religious buildings.

The **Fortress of Assenovgrad (Assenova Krepost)** has a fabled history of command and conquest, though its remains today are less than worthy of its past. The steep rocky hillside is a perfect position to guard the access to the Plain of Thrace and it was first used as a defensive bulwark by the Thracians, though the first substantial fortress was built during the reign of Tsar Ivan Assen II in the 13th century. The best preserved part is the **Petrich Church of the Virgin Mary** (Wed–Sun 8am–5pm), dominating the site.

Founded in 1083 by a Byzantine statesman of Georgian origin, the **Bachkovo Monastery** ⓯ (daily 7am–9pm, guides available 10am–4pm), 11km (7 miles) south of Assenovgrad, is a fine collection of well-preserved historic buildings from various eras. Highlights are the **refectory**, with frescoed walls depicting the monastery's history, and two churches, Sv Nikolai and the Church of the Virgin Mary, the oldest building

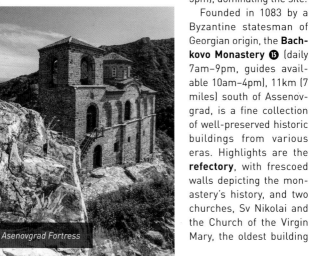

Asenovgrad Fortress

Bachkovo Monastery

in the monastery, dating from 1604. The Church of the Virgin Mary houses the **Icon of the Virgin**, supposed to have been brought from Georgia in 1310. Every year on St. Mary's Day, 15 August, it is paraded by thousands of pilgrims in a procession around the monastery.

CHEPELARE AND PAMPOROVO

An upgraded chair-lift has revolutionised the previously limited skiing at **Chepelare**, which looks set to become the country's next boom resort, although most visitors to this region still make a bee-line for **Pamporovo**, the most developed of Bulgaria's ski centres. A bus links the two resorts, which share a lift-pass. Pamporovo is great choice for families, it is far more suited to beginners than other Bulgarian resorts. The gentle slopes make for easy skiing (there is, however, one short black run called 'The Wall', recognised as the toughest piste in the country), and the ski-schools are excellent. While it offers a great choice of hotels, Pamporovo has nevertheless resisted the temptation to expand bed capacity too much. Lift queues here are short, even at weekends. During the summer Pamporovo is all but deserted, and makes a peaceful destination for gentle walks and fine air.

THE WESTERN RHODOPES

Heading west from Pamporovo – with a car preferably, as public transport in this remote part of Bulgaria is often non-existent – you enter an area populated almost entirely by a people known as the Pomaks, Bulgarians converted to Islam by the Turks in the 17th century. Though the occasional Christian village is dotted here and there, mosques dominate the landscape.

Shiroka Luka ⓰, a short distance from Pamporovo, is a village museum often full of package tourists from Pamporovo trying to get a feel of the real Bulgaria. Though short on individual attractions, apart from the **Church of the Assumption**,

---

⊙ BEARS

Bulgaria is home to approximately 750 brown bears, one of the largest populations in Europe. The majority live in the Rila and Rhodope mountains at an altitude of around 1,100m (3,600ft). Small numbers are hunted each year, though these are usually problem bears identified by the authorities as dangerous to the overall well-being of a group. The high charges paid by hunters also help to fund conservation programmes. Contact with people is extremely rare (about 150 cases each year), of which about a third end with bears attacking humans.

Church in Shiroka Laka

which has Zograf frescoes, the village is a delight to amble around, with cobbled streets, large Rhodope houses and picturesque courtyards. It is also a great place to witness the **Kukeri festival**, which takes place each year on the first Sunday of March (see page 96).

Passing through the spa town of **Devin**, most visitors head straight for the **Trigad Gorge**, a steep, narrow chasm cut by the lively River Trogradska. At the apex of the gorge the river plunges down into a cave known as the **Dyavolskoto Gurlo** or **Devil's Throat** ⑰ (Wed–Sun; guided tours only; charge discretional), one of the most spectacular natural sights in the country. A viewing platform has been positioned over the point where the river goes underground, while the tour of the cave, which is memorable for its sheer size and deafening echo of gushing water, is not for the faint-hearted. The village of **Trigrad** has little to recommend it, but it has a couple of good hotels that make it a popular base for hiking and caving. The neighbouring village of **Yagodina** is a major centre for Bulgarian caving.

A short drive or a long hike from Trigrad, heading back towards Devin and turning right shortly before the gorge, is the village of **Mugla**, which wouldn't figure on any map were it not for the annual **gaidi (bagpipe) festival** that takes place here each August.

THE EASTERN RHODOPES

The remote **Eastern Rhodopes** are best accessed via **Dimitrovgrad**, an hour's drive from Plovdiv. Along with Kraków's suburb of Nowa Huta in Poland, Dimitrovgrad shares the distinction of being an entirely planned socialist-realist city. Built in the 1950s, its wide boulevards and monumental apartments blocks are potholed and faded today, but the scale is a testament to the belief once placed in Communism.

Heading south into the mountains the pink **Kardzhali pyramids** greet visitors to the town of the same name. Just one of many weird rock formations in the once volcanic area, the pyramids (also known as the Svatba Vkamenenata, or Stone Wedding) are said to be a wedding party turned to stone by the gods to punish the bridegroom's mother for envying the bride's

The Kardzhali pyramids

beauty. **Kardzahli** is a nice enough town, but the only real sight is the **ruined fortress of Perperikon**, 20km (13 miles) northeast of town, where archaeologists have unearthed layers of civilisation going back some 7,000 years.

THE EASTERN BALKANS

Characterised by magnificent scenery and endless historical tales of heroism, liberation and derring-do, the Eastern Balkans form what is often described as both the cradle and the nursery of the Bulgarian nation. The magnificent fortress at Veliko Tarnovo defended one of the largest cities in -medieval Europe when it was capital of the Second Bulgarian Kingdom; monasteries were built in abundance – there are more than 40 in the region – and the largely unspoiled area remains today a symbol of national pride and togetherness.

VELIKO TARNOVO

The majestic capital of the Second Bulgarian Kingdom, **Veliko Tarnovo** ⑱ is one of the most picturesque cities in Bulgaria, mainly due to its setting on the steep banks of the Yantra River. Offering a good choice of accommodation, it is an excellent base from which to explore the historically significant surrounding area. The exquisite village of Arbanasi is close by, as is the Preobrazhenski Monastery, the finest and best preserved in the region.

At various times called Ternov, Trunov, Turnovgrad or simply Tarnovo, Veliko Tarnovo's existence has long depended on possession of the imposing citadel that sits atop **Tsaravets** (daily Apr–Sept 8am–7pm, Oct–Mar 10am–5pm), the highest of the three sacred hills among which the city nestles. The main attraction in Veliko Tarnovo, Tsaravets was first settled

Tsarevets Fortress

by the Thracians, though the first fortifications were probably constructed by the Byzantines in the 6th and 7th centuries. As the Byzantine Empire declined, that first fortress fell into ruins, which were built on in the 10th century by the Slavs, who were responsible for much of the structure that can be seen today. By the 12th century, the city was densely populated. Its position as the cradle of the nation was set in stone in 1187, when the successful rebellion of Peter and Assen against Byzantium was launched from Tsaravets, and Peter proclaimed a new Bulgarian Kingdom. Over the next 200 years the town flourished, until the summer of 1393 when, after a three-month siege, the overwhelmingly powerful Turkish army overran the citadel and set the town alight.

What remains of the fortress today is dominated by its restored **southern ramparts** and **Baldwin's Tower**, while the **Bulgarian Patriarchate**, with an orange exterior and green domes, towers above the ruins of the Tsar's Palace, which only hint at the size it must once have been.

A number of other churches surround the Tsaravets, the best preserved being the **Church of Peter and Paul** – at the foot of Tsaravet's northern slopes where the Yantra performs one of its many U-turns – and the **Church of the 40 Martyrs**, slightly further along Mitropolska towards Old Town.

Veliko Tarnovo's **Old Town** can become crowded with day-trippers, but it's usually a relaxed, even sleepy place, perfect for exploring on foot. Unfortunately, administrators of the three **museums (Archaeological**, **National Revival** and **History**; all daily 9am–6pm) in the centre fail to understand that non-Bulgarians may be interested in the country's history; all captions are in Bulgarian only and there are no guided tours.

From the Old Town, most visitors make their way up ul Jamiyata, which leads to pl Velchova Zavera and the **House of the Monkey**, so called because a tiny monkey statue sits below the first-floor bay window. The market in **pl Samodivska**, behind pl Velchova Zavera, is one of the best places in Bulgaria to find handmade pottery (see page 91).

From here begins **ul Stamboliski**, the city's primary commercial street, with shops, cafés and

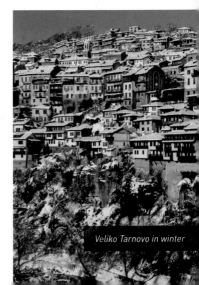

Veliko Tarnovo in winter

restaurants, a number of which have small terraces at the back that offer great views of the valley below. The **monument** in pl Pobornicheski marks the site where revolutionaries Bacho Kiro, Tsanko Dyustabanov and Georgi Izmirliev were hanged by the Turks in 1876. More shops, cafés and restaurants line the route towards **pl Nezavisimost**, the centre of modern Veliko Tarnovo.

The huge, orange building that dominates the lower part of Veliko Tarnovo is the **Boris Denev Art Gallery** (Tue–Sat 10am–6pm). The awful monument in front of it is a tribute to the Assen Dynasty, put up in the 1980s as part of the '1,300 years of Bulgaria' celebrations. Surrounding the art gallery is a shaded park with gentle paths perfect for afternoon strolls.

AROUND VELIKO TARNOVO

The village-museum of **Arbanasi** ⓲, a 10-minute drive uphill from Veliko Tarnovo, has more charms per square kilometre than any other village in Bulgaria. A flourishing trade and craft centre from the middle of the 16th century, the village is made up of monumental fortress-style houses and exquisite churches. The best of these is the **Church of the Archangels Michael and Gabriel** on a small hill above the village's park, and the **Kostantsialev House** (Tue–Sun 9am–6pm) on the other side of the park. In all, there are five house-museums and four churches, as well as two rather plain monasteries.

Returning to Veliko Tarnovo and taking the main road for Ruse, the **Preobrazhensk Monastery** is situated about 6km (4 miles) north of the town. One of many monasteries in the area founded in the 14th century, it flourished during the Second Bulgarian Kingdom only to be burnt by the Turks after they had taken Veliko Tarnovo. Rebuilt in the 19th

Preobrazhensky Monastery

century during the National Revival, it is a fine example of the era's architecture and iconography. The central **Church of the Transfiguration** includes two characteristic frescoes by Zahari Zograf, the *Last Judgement* and the *Wheel of Life*. There are two other churches in the monastery, the **Church of the Annunciation**, with icons by Stanislav Dospevski, and the **Church of the Ascension**. The **bell** in the courtyard's bell tower was a gift from Russia's Tsar Alexander II.

South of Veliko Tarnovo is the equally remarkable **Kilifarevo Monastery**. Founded by Teodisil Turnovski as a centre of Hesychasm, a religious doctrine that preached unity with God through isolation, it was another monastery burnt to the ground by the Turks in the late 14th century, only to be refounded and rebuilt in the 19th century. Its impressive central church, the **Church of Sv Dimitar**, includes a stunning portrait of St John of Rila by Kristu Zahariev.

SOUTH OF VELIKO TARNOVO

Southwest of Veliko Tarnovo towards Kazanlak is the small town of **Dryanovo**, another town associated with rebellion and nationalism. Dating back to the 12th century, the town's **Monastery**, 4km (2 miles) further on, was the site of an anti-Turkish uprising in 1876, when 220 revolutionaries led by Bacho Kiro held a large Turkish army at bay for nine days before the Turks blew the monastery up and hanged the rebels in Veliko Tarnovo. Most of the monastery's buildings were fully restored after liberation. Just beyond the monastery is the floodlit **Bacho Kiro Cave** (daily during the summer, irregular hours), a good opportunity to see stalactites and stalagmites.

Climbing steadily into the Balkans, **Gabrovo**, gateway to the Shipka Pass, is a former textile town with little to offer except

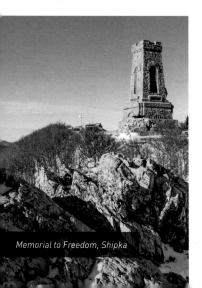

Memorial to Freedom, Shipka

a **Museum of Humour and Satire** (ul Bryanska 64; Apr–Oct daily 9am–6pm, Nov–Mar Mon–Sat 9am–6pm) and a festival in May in odd-numbered years, the **International Biennial of Humour and Satire**. The museum and festival are in Gabrovo because it is the traditional butt of most Bulgarian jokes, usually involving mean-ness and stupidity. Some 8km (5 miles) southeast of the town is **Etura** (daily 8am–6pm), a craft cen-tre set up to preserve the town's traditional skills. The complex's houses, workshops and mills recreate with astonishing realism what life was like in Gabrovo 150 years ago.

South of Gabrovo is the stunning **Shipka Pass** ❷⓿, equal in majesty to the Iskar Gorge and every bit as deserving of its legendary status among local people. It was here that Alexander the Great won one of his first major victories as Macedonian leader in 335 BC and where – more importantly for Bulgarians – in August 1877 a Bulgarian and Russian force held back 30,000 Turks, thus allowing Pleven to be taken by other Bulgarian and Russian forces. Today, at the 1,326m (4,350ft) summit of Mt Stoletov, you will find the **Memorial to Freedom**, which is accessible from the road by 894 steps. The memorial houses a small museum (9am–5pm) dedicated to the battle. Beyond the apex of the pass, the village of **Shipka** is home to the splendid, pink, white and golden-domed **Shipka Memorial Church**, built in 1902 to commemorate the battle.

KAZANLAK AND STARA ZAGORA

During the first weekend of June each year, the town of **Kazanlak** holds the **Festival of the Roses**, an age-old pageant celebrating the rose harvest of the surrounding villages, which together form what Bulgarians refer to as the **Valley of the Roses**. The roses are in full bloom during the late spring. Kazanlak became rich on its rose oil during the 18th century, and today the **Museum of the Rose** (daily 9am–5.30pm) in Tyubelto Park tells the story.

The biggest draw in town, however, is the **Thracian Tomb**, also in Tyubelto Park, dating from the 4th century BC and excavated in 1944. So precious is Bulgaria's finest surviving example of Thracian art that the tomb is closed to the public. The **replica** (daily 9am–5pm) next to it is a perfect reproduction of the original in every respect, from the red floors to the stunning frescoes on the domed ceiling.

Situated in the geographical centre of Bulgaria, **Stara Zagora** is one of the country's largest cities. Founded as Beroe in the 6th century BC by the Thracians it became the Roman town Augusta Traiana, the Byzantine town Irinopolis and the Turkish town Eski Zaara, before being completely destroyed by the Turks during the war of liberation. After independence it was rebuilt following a grid system devised by the Czech urban planner Lubor Bayer. As with most planned towns, Stara Zagora lacks character and has little to offer the visitor except the **Bereketska Mogila Neolithic Dwellings** (Tue–Sun 9am–noon, 2–5pm; English guided tours), the largest prehistoric settlement unearthed in Bulgaria. The dwellings date from at least 5500 BC and provide a fascinating insight into the life of the ancient people who lived in them.

⊘ ROSE OIL

Bulgaria has been one of the world's leading producers of rose oil since the 18th century, when Turkish traders noticed that the area around Kazanlak (now known as the Valley of the Roses) would be perfect for cultivating the flower. Harvesting the rose is a race against time, as the flower must be picked before 9am, when it is still wet with dew. The harvest must then be rushed to the distillery before the oil has evaporated. Bulgarian steam-distilled rose oil, 100 percent pure, is today recognised as being the finest – and most expensive – in the world, and is used in the production of perfumes, as well as in meditation. The Festival of the Roses is celebrated every June in Kazanlak.

THE BLACK SEA

Of all Bulgaria's charms as a holiday destination, it is the fantastic beaches and warm waters of the Black Sea that have been attracting tourists the longest. From brash Sunny Beach to chic Albena, from enchanting Balchick to bewitching Nessebur, Bulgaria's 400km (249 miles) of coastline offer everything: golden sands, rocky coves, nature reserves and

Hotel complex in Albena on the Black Sea

delightful fishing villages. The region can be rough around the edges: the transport infrastructure is poor (particularly the roads), customer service can be under par, and many resorts are blighted by construction sites. But for a great-value summer holiday there is nowhere in Europe to match Bulgaria's Black Sea coast. To get the best of it, spend a week or two at one of the many good hotels in the major beach resorts of Golden Sands or Sunny Beach, but don't neglect to visit the real gems: little Nessebur and ancient Sozopol.

VARNA

The third-largest city in Bulgaria, **Varna** ㉑ is part seaport and part beach resort. It has a mish-mash of cultures and architectural styles and a brashness that characterises most Black Sea towns and cities. Most of the thousands of tourists who come here on package tours head straight to the nearby resorts of Golden Sands and Albena, but Varna itself is definitely worth a look: a city of 350,000 that offers a vibrant café and restaurant scene, great museums, a rich cultural heritage and one of the finest operas in Bulgaria. It is also the best place to shop, outside the capital. Like much of the Black Sea coast, however, Varna remains a little tatty around the edges.

Although there was once an ancient Thracian settlement close by, the city dates from the 6th century BC, when Greek colonists founded the little settlement of Odessos, which quickly became an important centre of trade and fishing. Conquered in turn by Alexander the Great and the Romans, the city flourished under both of these empires until Barbarians destroyed it in 586. Repopulated by the Slavs, who gave the town its present name, Varna remained a city on the fringes until the 19th century when it became the most important sea port within the newly independent Bulgaria.

Pl Nezavisimost, Varna's pedestrianised central square, surrounded on all sides by terraces and cafés in the summer, is dominated by the shocking-pink, 19th-century **Varna Opera House and Philharmonia**, and the **Old Clock Tower**, dating from 1880. Across the main boulevard, Hristo

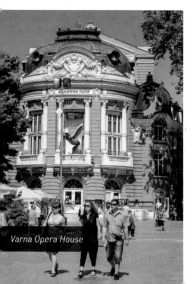
Varna Opera House

Botev, stands the 19th-century **Cathedral of the Holy Virgin Ⓐ**, more impressive from afar than it is close up. The interior is spectacular – the icons and frescoes took 25 years to complete – but the exterior is in need of repair and you will be asked to make a donation, before

A town called Stalin

From 1947–56 Varna was officially named Stalin in honour of the Soviet leader. A number of other cities in Eastern Europe, including Brasov in Romania, suffered a similar fate.

being blessed, as you make your way inside. A good market, selling local embroidery and lace along with the usual souvenirs, surrounds the cathedral.

From here, a short walk along the pleasantly wide **Maria Luiza Boulevard** brings you to the **Varna Archaeological Museum Ⓑ** (daily 10am–5pm), the city's best museum. Set in splendid gardens, it was built as a school during the National Revival. Various exhibits vie for your attention, including miniature models of Palaeolithic pile dwellings, ancient art and jewellery, and various ancient Egyptian, Greek and even Babylonian artefacts.

The awful skyscraper on the other side of the road is the Town Hall. Just north of here, on Rakovski Boulevard, is the Church of Sv Petka, famous for its striped walls and marvellous central cupola. To the south of the Town Hall is the **Art Gallery** (Tue–Sun 10am–6pm), which houses a fine collection of Bulgarian and foreign art.

From the art gallery, it is a short walk to **Knyaz Boris I Boulevard**, the city's main thoroughfare and shopping street, which buzzes from morning until late at night throughout the summer. A short distance along this pedestrianised street is the **Sv Nikola Church**, which was built in 1866 and contains icons by many of the finest Bulgarian masters, though much of the church is inaccessible at present due to restoration work. Just round the corner is the **National Revival Museum**  (ul 27 Yuli; Mon–Fri 10am–5pm), a church and Varna's first Bulgarian school, which became a museum in 1959. The story of the city's history and liberation is told, in English and Bulgarian, in well-preserved classrooms.

Heading towards the port along Han Krum, the **Church of Sv Bogodoritsa** looms on the left. This was built in the 17th century according to Turkish rules that limited the height of churches, hence its sunken foundations and afterthought of a tower. On the other side of the road are the **Roman Thermae** (Tue–Sat 10am–5pm), built in the 2nd century and abandoned to the Barbarians in the 6th century. After much restoration

The municipal beach, Primorski Park

work, the baths are now one of the city's most important archaeological sights. Almost adjacent to the Thermae is the **Church of Sv Atanasii**, a fine example of National Revival architecture. Another classic of the National Revival period houses the **Ethnographic Museum** Ⓔ (Apr–Oct daily 10am–5pm, Nov–Mar Tue–Sun 10am–5pm). Exhibits include various Kukeri masks, making this a good opportunity for travellers not fortunate enough to experience a Kukeri festival to see just how bizarre these events are (see page 96).

PRIMORSKI PARK

The huge **Primorski Park** Ⓕ, stretching from Varna's port almost to the pleasant, tiny beach resort of **Sv Konstantin**, took years to lay out and was finally completed in 1908. It is very popular with local people, who flock here to sunbathe on Varna's excellent municipal **beach** or attend pop and rock concerts throughout the summer at the **open-air theatre**. The numerous terraces, pubs and discos lining the beach front are full most nights all summer long.

The park has various attractions, some of dubious quality. Like the park itself, both the **Naval Museum** (daily 9am–5pm) with naval hardware, at the far western end of the park, and the **Aquarium and Black Sea Museum** (June–Sept 9am–7pm, Oct–May 9am–5pm) have seen better days, but both remain favourites with children. Also popular with children are the **Planetarium** (June–Sept 9am–3.30pm, shows every 90 minutes; Oct–May by prior appointment) and the **Dolphinarium** (shows at 10.30, noon, 3.30pm, 5pm) at the other end of the park. The **Zoo** (May–Sept daily 8am–8pm, Oct–Apr daily 8.30am–4.30pm) in the middle of the park features a large number of animals including camels, emus and other exotic birds, spiders, snakes, crabs, frogs, geckos and rodents.

GOLDEN SANDS

Known to Bulgarians as Zlatni Pyusatsi, **Golden Sands** is a sprawling, purpose-built seaside resort 18km (11 miles) north of Varna. A staple of Western European holiday brochures, it is the best known of all the Bulgarian beach resorts. Always make sure you have accommodation booked before arriving, as hotel rack rates are far higher than those offered by online booking companies and tour operators. At busy times the resort can often be full.

Although perhaps not quite golden, the 5km (3-mile) beach is fabulous, sloping gently to the sea, and offering every water sport from parascending and water-skiing to jet-skiing and windsurfing at various points along its length. The resort's small marina is at the northern end of the resort, beyond which is a nudist beach. There is a water park, **Aquapolis**, behind the resort on the other side of the main road from Varna to Balchik.

There are more than 70 hotels of all categories in the resort, all now in private hands and fully refurbished. Not all of the resort's hotels are on the seafront, however, and some are quite a way from the beach. Though there is no real centre to this artificial resort, there is a collection of shops and banks around the **Church of St John**.

There are plenty of good restaurants and cheap places to eat throughout the resort, and an endless number of bars and discos. Both the Havan and International hotels have casinos. The resort is linked to Varna by

Aladzha Monastery

In a forest northwest of Golden Sands are the remains of the rock-hewn Aladzha Monastery (Tue–Sun 9am–6pm), founded in the 14th century and populated by the Hesychast order of monks until the 18th century. There is a small museum that shows how the monastery looked when it was occupied.

numerous taxis (make sure you take a taxi displaying the name and phone number of a taxi company), and by bus numbers 109 and 409. The journey takes about 20 minutes one-way.

ALBENA

The trendiest, and consequently most expensive, of the Black Sea resorts, **Albena**, 30km (18 miles) from Varna, is smaller than Golden Sands and a lot younger; until 1970 there

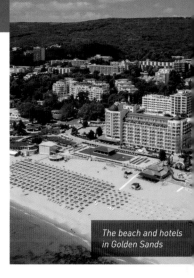

The beach and hotels in Golden Sands

wasn't a hotel in sight. Today the step-pyramid conceptual creations come as something of a pleasant surprise after the straight lines of Golden Sands. The resort is increasingly popular with Bulgaria's smart set and less frequented by foreign tourists.

The beach itself is wider, whiter and quieter than Golden Sands, though there is less scope for water sports. There is an excellent **equestrian centre** next to the Malibu Hotel, which offers riding lessons and horse-back excursions into the surrounding countryside.

BALCHIK

The fact that the small town of **Balchik**, 15km (10 miles) north of Albena, was made famous by Romania's Queen Marie, Queen Victoria's granddaughter, who had her summer residence here, highlights the difficult history of the Dobruja region. Lost to Romania after the Balkan Wars, Balchik and the rest

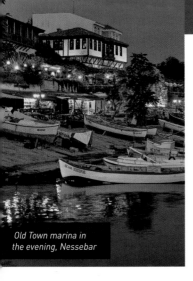
Old Town marina in the evening, Nessebar

of the Dobruja was only returned to Bulgaria by Hitler in 1940. Since then it has become a popular resort with Bulgarians and Romanians, who find the place a quiet retreat. Balchik is also home to three championship-standard links golf courses.

The main attraction remains the **Tenha Yuva** complex (8am–5pm, gardens until 9pm in summer) the palace of Queen Marie. The simple palace itself, set on a hilltop overlooking the town, is dominated by a minaret-like tower and betrays Marie, who insisted on designing almost every detail herself, as a rather unsophisticated architect. A number of other buildings are far lovelier, including a stone summer house from where the queen watched the sea. The botanical gardens are home to more than 3,000 rare and exotic plants. Some 4km (2 miles) from Balchik is **Tuzlata**, a tiny resort famous for its mud treatments. At Dabolka, the Black Sea's biggest mussel farm serves thousands of huge pots of steaming mussels every day.

BOURGAS AND SURROUNDINGS

The largest town on the southern part of the coast, the important port and industrial city of **Bourgas**, has little to offer the visitor and, with the far more attractive towns of -Pomorie, Nessebur and Sozopol all close by, it should be used only as a stopping-off point or day trip destination at best.

Pomorie, around 20km (13 miles) northeast of Bourgas, is situated on a slim, rocky peninsula separating the bay of Bourgas from the Black Sea, and has been offering mud treatments for well over 2,000 years. All the town's hotels double as mud treatment centres, and it is difficult to find a room unless you are booked into one of the clinics. Besides mud, the town is known for salt – and wine; Pamid, Dimyat and Merlots are among the country's best. Though narrow and often very crowded, the beach is excellent.

NESSEBUR

A further 18km (11 miles) north is **Nessebur** ㉒, which has Bulgaria's best beach and some of its best preserved 19th-century wooden architecture. Split in two by a slim causeway, Nessebur is famous mainly for its old town, situated on the peninsula that juts awkwardly into the Black Sea. The town's narrow, cobbled streets, wooden houses and medieval churches make it as much an emblem of Bulgaria as Dubrovnik is of Croatia.

Entering Old Nessebur via its **Town Gate**, with **fortifications** dating back to the 6th century on either side, it is possible to imagine how impregnable the town must have been. Once inside, the **Archaeological Museum** (Dec–Apr and Nov Mon–Fri 9am–5pm, May, Oct and Sept until 6pm, June until 7pm, July–Aug until 8pm; Sat–Sun Mar–May and Oct–Nov 10am–5pm, June 9.30am–2pm and 2.30–7pm, July–Sept 9am–1.30pm and 2–7pm), on the right as you enter, is a good introduction to the town's history. From there, magnificent **churches** await exploration; there were once more than 40 on the

Best for seafood

Nessebur, at the centre of the Bulgarian Black Sea's fishing industry, is the best place on the coast to enjoy seafood.

peninsula and many remain worthy of your time today. Following a roughly clockwise route around the peninsula, the first one that you will see is the 14th-century **Church of the Holy Pantocrator**, whose exterior marks it out as one of the finest medieval churches in the country. Next is the **Church of St John the Baptist**, an 11th-century structure caught between the simple designs of the early Christians and the more complex, ornate churches that followed. Following ul Alehoi, the next church you encounter is the 14th-century **Church of Archangels Michael and Gabriel**, a stunning example of medieval craftsmanship, while next to that is the less impressive **Church of Sv Paraskeva** of the same era. Further on is the **Church of Sv Bogodoritsa**, while on the seashore are the ruins of the **Basilica**, which date from the 5th century.

Inland, in the middle of the endlessly busy central square, **pl Mitropolitska**, the 5th-century **Old Bishopric (Sv Sofia)** stands in ruins, while its counterpart, the **New Bishopric (Sv Stefan)** on ul Rilbarska, is a much-rebuilt church dating from the 11th century. The frescoes date from the 17th century, the pulpit and bishop's throne from the 18th century. The 14th-century **Church of St John Aliturgitus** at the end of the same street is the best of Nessebur's churches. Perched high above the harbour, its bizarre exterior tops anything else in the town.

SUNNY BEACH

Just north of Nessebur is the lively beach resort of **Sunny Beach** (Slanchev Bryag). More than 150 hotels stretch along the narrow 7km (4-mile) beach, making the largest resort on the Black Sea. Having played second fiddle to Golden Sands for some time, Sunny Beach has had a revival and the completion of the Sofia–Burgas motorway has seen it become increasingly popular amongst Bulgarian families. It remains cheaper than the northern resorts, and offers great opportunities for water sports, while boasting some of the best value hotels on the coast. There are numerous restaurants and an endless number of bars and discos.

SOZOPOL

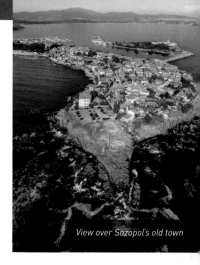

View over Sozopol's old town

Approximately 30km (21 miles) south of Bourgas, **Sozopol** ㉓, just about the last town on the coast, could well be the best. An ancient fishing village on a peninsula, much like Nessebur, Sozopol's distance from a large package holiday resort means that it does not get the day-trippers that crowd Nessebur, making it a far better place to wander around.

Like Nessebur, Sozopol is divided into old and new parts, Old Sozopol, on the peninsula, being the most popular destination for visitors. The causeway that links the two parts acts as the town's unofficial centre, and it is always awash with hawkers selling less-than-impressive souvenirs.

The rather ordinary **Archaeological Museum** (Mon–Fri 10am–5pm) stands on the south of the causeway. To the right is a small park containing two of Sozopol's Revival-period churches, the **Church of Sv Zosim** and the **Church of Sts Cyril and Methodius**, below which is the private Raiski Beach. **Old Sozopol** is a warren of narrow cobbled streets, wooden houses, churches, cafés, restaurants and souvenir shops. Every September Sozopol hosts the Apollonia Arts Festival, with opera, classical music and theatre, during which the town is swamped with visitors.

Chairlift at the Bansko ski resort

 **WHAT TO DO**

SPORTS AND OUTDOOR PURSUITS

SKIING

Bulgaria has been a popular destination for budget-conscious skiers for three decades. The main resorts are Borovets, Pamporovo and Bansko, while it is also possible to ski at Vitosha, just a bus ride from the centre of Sofia.

There is usually good snow cover in all of the resorts from late December to the end of March, and you can often ski on the highest slopes at Vitosha and Bansko well into April. While Bulgaria's skiing is good, however, it is not particularly extensive or challenging. As a rule of thumb, Pamporovo is best suited to beginners, Borovets and Bansko for intermediate skiers, while Vitosha offers the most difficult slopes in the country.

Vitosha apart, all the resorts are well appointed with a variety of hotels, self-catering apartments and places to hire ski equipment. You will pay far more if arriving on spec than if you book accommodation and ski hire before departure. Lift pass prices are increasing, although they are still very low by western European standards – around 35 leva per day. Ski schools are also cheap, and invariably very good. Indeed, for absolute beginners, there are few better places In Europe to learn how to ski or snowboard.

All of Bulgaria's ski resorts get crowded at the weekends and public holidays when city-dwellers swarm all over them. Vitosha, just 15km (10 miles) from Sofia, is the worst affected, so expect long queues and crowded pistes on Saturday and Sunday. During the week, however, at all of the resorts you may well have the slopes to yourself.

HIKING AND WALKING

As spring gives way to summer, skiers give way to hikers and walkers, both local people and international tourists. Unpredictable weather in late spring can mean that snow and freezing temperatures grip the mountains as late as the end of May. The season begins in earnest in June.

Hiking is one of the most popular activities in the country, so hikers are well catered for. The best areas are the Pirin, Rila and Rhodope mountains, all three ranges offering a large number of well-marked routes. For longer hikes you will need to be in possession of a good map before setting off. These can be bought in all good bookshops in Sofia, or in hotels in mountain resorts. Always check weather conditions before heading off; even in high summer the weather can turn in an instant at high altitude.

Most routes are dotted with small cabins – usually open only in summer – where you can buy refreshments and sometimes spend the night for just a few leva.

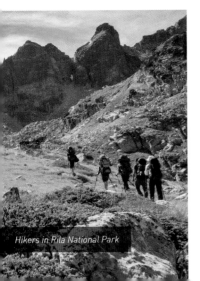

Hikers in Rila National Park

MOUNTAIN BIKING

Mountain biking is relatively new in Bulgaria, as is biking of any sort. There are a number of marked tracks laid out for mountain bikers, the best at Pamporovo, Borovets and Bansko. Unless you bring your own bike, head for one of these ski resorts, where you will be able to rent a bike in good condition from a hotel, such as the Rila or Samokov in Borovets, the Pamporovo or Finlandia in Pamporovo, or Pirin or Bansko in Bansko.

GOLF

Golf is perhaps the fastest growing sport in Bulgaria, and the country now offers ten full 18-hole courses (there were none a decade or so ago The closest course to the capital is the par-72 St Sofia Golf Club and Spa, 25km (15 miles) east of the capital (www.stsofiagolf.com). There are three par-72 courses in and around Balchik on the Black Sea, with par-71 courses at Sliven and Ihtiman, 50km (30 miles) from Sofia along the Sofia–Plovdiv highway. There are two courses near Borovets, and two near Bansko, including the Ian Woosnam-designed course at the Pirin Golf Club (www.piringolf.bg), regarded as the best in the country. Golf is competitively-priced, if far from cheap, and all ten courses are open to the general public. Expect to pay from 60 leva for a round (more at weekends). All clubs now have resident pros offering lessons.

SAILING

Increasingly popular among the nouveaux riches, leisure sailing is centred on Golden Sands, and there are 11 marinas along the coast. The most popular are the Golden Sands Marina, Port Varna Marina Club and the Bourgas Yacht Club. All have boats for hire, but you will need proof of your sailing credentials.

FOOTBALL

Bulgarians are mad about football, which remains the most popular spectator sport by some way. The country's finest hour came in 1994 when the national team – led by the legendary

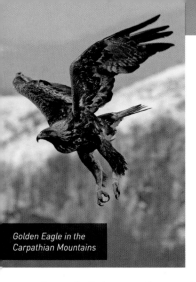

Golden Eagle in the Carpathian Mountains

Hristo Stoichkov – narrowly lost to Italy in the World Cup semi-final. Since then, Bulgarian football has been in steady decline. The national team has failed to qualify for a major tournament since the 2004 European Championships, and with the current crop of local talent not considered particularly good, it may be some time before Bulgaria is ready to take its place at football's top table again.

Domestically, however, the game is in surprisingly good shape, with crowds at big games up on those in recent years. Matches between the country's biggest and most popular sides (Levski and CSKA Sofia, Ludogorets Razgrad and Lokomotiv Plovdiv) are usually sell-outs, and are well worth attending if you can get a ticket. The Bulgarian season runs from July to June, with a break from December to March.

HUNTING

Bulgaria's varied countryside presents opportunities to hunt big and small game, including deer, wild boar, bears, pheasants, ducks and partridges. The rules governing the sport are strict, with annual quotas for each species. Payment is determined by species and size. Shooting a pheasant may cost just a few leva, while hunting a large brown bear may cost thousands of euros. Hunters need an international hunting licence (or at least a hunting license from their home country) and must have special permits to bring their guns into the country.

If you want to hunt in Bulgaria, it is best to have a local travel agent take care of all the paperwork. A number of travel agents specialise in hunting holidays, including Sofia-based BHS (www.huntservice.com).

FISHING

Fishing is popular all over the country. Freshwater fishing is especially good in the Rila Mountains where, depending on the season, you can find carp, mullet, pike and pike-perch, with only May (the spawning season) off-limits. The Black Sea offers huge numbers of saltwater fish, including turbot, mackerel and tunny fish. There is no angling off-season on the coast. A small dog shark is also found in the Black Sea and it can be fished from a boat around 4km (2 miles) off the coast. Most Sofia tour agencies can make arrangements for angling safaris.

BIRDWATCHING

Once a well-kept secret, Bulgaria's reputation for birdwatching has become more widely known in recent years, and the country is fast becoming one of Europe's top birdwatching destinations. Two areas in particular offer a great range of bird species: the marshlands around Bourgas and the Madzharovo nature reserve in the Rhodope Mountains. The more than 500 kinds of bird that either nest in Bulgaria in spring or pass through on migration in the autumn, include the Dalmatian pelican, glossy ibis, spoonbill, black stork, pygmy cormorant, ferruginous duck, Egyptian, black and griffon vultures, Levant sparrow-hawk, long-legged buzzard, peregrine falcon and white-tailed, golden and eastern imperial eagles.

Among the tour operators offering birdwatching excursions is Sofia-based Pandion (www.birdwatchingholidays.com), which can help with all aspects of birdwatching, from booking hotels to tailor-made, fully escorted tours. Pandion also offers butterfly and dragon-fly-spotting tours. Independent birdwatchers should come in spring to Pamporovo, a good base in the Rhodopes, and to Bourgas in the autumn. Even the casual observer will, however, notice a profusion of birdlife at any time of year in almost any rural setting.

SHOPPING

Bulgaria is by no means a shopper's paradise, but it does offer some of the best shopping in the Balkans. During the Communist period there wasn't much to interest anyone, and while Bulgarian shops were never as barren and depressingly deserted as their Romanian counterparts, it was still difficult to purchase many consumer goods without having to wait for some time. All that has changed. Economic reform may not have been as fast as that of other former Communist countries, but when it comes to consumer commerce, the Bulgarians now lead the way.

In the days of the 'wild East' – immediately following the collapse of the Communist regime – almost anything could be bought for any price. Although those days have gone, you will still find a few forbidden fruits in the country's flea markets, most notably counterfeit CDs and DVDs, production of which is one of the country's biggest industries (see page 92).

Shops in general are open all day until around 6pm. Note that customer service is still non-existent. Credit cards are now accepted in all but the smallest stores, although using one invariably provokes muttering.

MARKETS AND MALLS

Prices in general can be divided into two categories: cheap (if the product is made in Bulgaria) and expensive (if the product is imported). While haggling has long been a Balkan necessity, it is now frowned upon in all but the most provincial markets. Try it in a chic boutique in Sofia and the police may be called.

Most of Bulgaria's groceries are still purchased early in the morning at markets, and produce is strictly seasonal. Imported goods can be found out of season only in expensive supermarkets. Almost everything else is sold in standard high-street shops or malls. The biggest is Mall of Sofia, which also boasts the only IMAX cinema in the country. There are also a number of flea markets for those who know where to look. The biggest and best is the one in front of the Alexander Nevski Cathedral

Souvenir stalls on Ploshtad Nikola Vaptsarov, Bansko

in Sofia. If you are looking for a genuine Third Reich fountain pen, then this is the place to come, while busts of Lenin and Stalin and posters of Todor Zhivkov and other Communist heroes are also popular. Russian army hats are two a penny, while medals, watches and other Soviet memorabilia – all of which may or may not be original – can be bought for peanuts. Directly next to the flea market is another one, selling Orthodox iconography and naive art which, while not cheap, is good quality and a very good place to hunt for souvenirs.

The Black Sea coast's numerous street hawkers sell little else but sunglasses, beachwear and accessories, most of which is terribly poor in terms of quality. Ski resorts attract the winter equivalent of these hawkers. Sports shops in the ski resorts can offer bargain ski equipment, as a number of Western brands manufacture in Bulgaria under licence, and prices for skis and ski boots are much cheaper here than in Western Europe, especially after the end of February.

WHAT TO BUY

Traditional Bulgarian handicrafts offer a wide choice of wares. These include lace, pottery, woodcarvings and iconography. Bulgarian souvenir shops are ubiquitous, though the souvenirs themselves can be of variable quality.

Reproductions of **Orthodox iconography** and **wood carvings** can be bought all over the country, with the best quality being found in Sofia in the art market outside the Alexander Nevski Cathedral. As a general rule, the stuff sold by hawkers and stallholders outside the more famous Bulgarian monasteries should be bought only in a souvenir emergency, as quality is patchy at best.

If you are after **genuine antique icons**, as opposed to reproductions, you should contact a professional art dealer and have a reasonable idea of what you are looking for. Exporting antiques is a difficult process requiring a long paper chase that a dealer will be able to handle with ease. Only the brave should attempt to do it on their own. There are a number of galleries in Sofia clustered together on the streets around the Radisson Hotel. Any of them will be delighted to help.

The manufacture of **fine pottery** in this part of the world dates back as far as the Thracians, and the work of Bulgarian potters is traditionally sacred, with know-how a closely guarded secret kept within families of potters. Pottery first flourished during the 12th to 14th centuries, only to go into abeyance during the Turkish Yoke, before being resurrected during the National Revival period. This is when Berkovitsa and Gabrovo became bywords for excellence in the field, their green, brown and yellow creations a Bulgarian trademark. Over the last hundred years or so the craft has somewhat died out, and today only a few potteries remain, mostly as working museums. The **Etura complex** near Gabrovo (see page 68) is a fine example of this kind of living museum and an excellent place to purchase exquisite handmade Bulgarian pottery, as is the market in pl Samodivska in **Veliko Tarnovo**.

Icons for sale in Sofia

Etura is also a good location to find **embroidery and lace**, though the best place is probably along the coast, especially in Varna, as there is so much choice and competition between the old ladies who throng the market that surrounds the Cathedral of the Virgin Mary. Quality here is high and prices are reasonable, though not cheap. You can try haggling but few of these *babushki* speak any English, and may not understand your attempts to get the price of an item down.

WHERE TO SHOP

Sofia. Vitosha Boulevard is the country's top shopping street, though you will not find anything here that cannot be bought (often cheaper) in your home country. The best souvenir shops in the capital are those on the second floor of the TZUM department store and in the underpass leading from the Presidency to the Largo. The Halite grocery market can be fun in the early mornings, while the Zhenski Pazar (Women's Market) is

☉ FAKING IT

Bulgaria remains one of the world's largest producers of fake CDs and DVDs, despite repeated calls from the European Union to stamp out their production, retail and export. The government makes occasional high-profile raids on illegal factories, but these do little real damage to what is a multi-billion euro industry. All Bulgarian towns and cities are full of street retailers brazenly offering discs for sale, usually a mind-boggling selection of the most up-to-date music, as well as back-catalogues. In most cases if the vendor does not have the particular album you are looking for, he will have one made for you overnight.

another good place to hunt for bargains. Graf Ignatiev Boulevard is home to an excellent second-hand book market, as well as an outlet for counterfeit CDs and DVDs. There are now also two big modern malls in Sofia: the Mall of Sofia, on the city's outskirts, and City Center Sofia, closer to the centre of town.

Book market in Sofia

Plovdiv. The pedestrian only Alexander I Boulevard, which leads from pl Tsentralen towards Old Plovdiv, is the city's foremost shopping throughfare, and has numerous cafés, restaurants and bars. There is an excellent daily market situated on ul Raichio, on the southern side of pl Tsentralen, where good, cheap forgeries of all your favourite brand-name clothes are a speciality.

Varna. Knyaz Boris I Boulevard, from pl Nezavisimost to Tsar Osvoboditel Boulevard, has perhaps the best selection of shops anywhere in Bulgaria. All the major international brand names have boutiques on the street, and these often sit side by side with discount stores selling counterfeit versions of the same goods. Varna is also home to a number of nautical shops, some selling tacky souvenirs, others selling professional sailing gear. The market outside the cathedral is the best place in the country to find lace and embroidery, although the flea market situated on the other side of the main road sells only rubbish to tourists who should know better.

ENTERTAINMENT

NIGHTLIFE AND CAFÉ CULTURE

Bulgaria is now one of Europe's best places for good value night-life. Sophisticated clubs and discos come and go (especially on the coast) with startling regularity, opening up in a blaze of glory before closing just months later as the country's hip crowd moves on to somewhere new. There is something for all tastes and pockets: from the brash discos to smooth jazz cafés and Irish pubs.

Given its sheer size and wide choice of bars and discos, Sofia is probably best for nightlife, while all the Black Sea resorts, especially Golden Sands and Sunny Beach, have a reputation for long, long nights and also have a number of casinos. Varna, too, has a profusion of good discos along its seafront. The ski resorts, catering mainly for foreign tourists, also have good night-time options, while the student town of Blagoevgrad is a major nightlife centre for the young during term-time.

CULTURAL PERFORMANCES

The cultural capital of the country remains Plovdiv, where the Roman Amphitheatre stages world-class music and theatre

Gaida players at a festival in Rozhen

throughout the summer. Varna also has a number of festivals, including the Varna International Pop Music Festival, held at various venues throughout the city every May, with performers of variable ability, though there is usually at least one major international star. Far more satisfactory is the Varna Classical Summer Festival, held every June and featuring big names from the world of Bulgarian and international music and opera.

The Sofia National Opera is the country's most famous opera, though the standard of performances depends on the singers on stage on any particular night, as those most in demand are often performing elsewhere.

There are good operas at Blagoevgrad, Varna and Plovdiv. The country's best performers congregate at Plovdiv in the summer when they perform at the amphitheatre. Tickets are invariably cheap and represent excellent value for money.

FOLK MUSIC

Among connoisseurs, traditional Bulgarian music – especially female singing – is respected and renowned worldwide. It may well be one day enjoyed in other galaxies – one of the *Voyager* rockets launched in the 1970s, in the hope of it eventually being picked up by other life forms, includes a Bulgarian folk song from the Rhodopes on a gilded copper gramophone record.

To hear Bulgarian music closer to earth, you should head for the Pirin Song Festival held every August, or buy any of the excellent compilation cassettes and CDs of Bulgarian music that can be found in music stores and souvenir shops.

Traditional instruments include the *gaida* (bagpipes), the *kaval* (shepherd's pipes), the *brumbuzuk* (a small pipe) and *chans* (sheep's bells). All are impossibly difficult to play but make extraordinary music when performed well. One of the best places to see traditional music being performed is at any restaurant offering a folk programme. Though often designed for tourists, they are usually very good value.

CHILDREN'S BULGARIA

Bulgaria's seaside and ski resorts are terrific destinations for families, as accommodation is excellent value and children's activities are relatively cheap. There are water parks up and down the Black Sea coast, with plenty of places to swim or try water sports. Do be careful when taking part in any water sports, however, as not all sports centres have the correct authorisation. It is best to head for an activity centre attached to a good hotel. Shows at the dolphinarium in Varna are popular

⊙ KUKERI FESTIVALS

Almost certainly Thracian in origin, the Kukeri festivals are probably the most bewildering sights in Bulgaria for the uninitiated. At various times throughout the year – usually at New Year or in spring – participants (always male) dress up in animal skins – including elaborate, fearsome masks often made from animal heads – and enter a trance-like state before parading through towns and villages manically chanting, dancing, shouting, singing, and generally acting in a way that will make evil spirits think twice before returning. The parades can last all day and mock executions are often enacted to symbolise the death of winter.

As recently as the 19th century, the tradition was common all over the country but today just a few large Kukeri festivals remain. The best places to see them are Pernik, a small town 25km (15 miles) west of Sofia, during the last weekend of January; and Shiroka Luka, close to Pamporovo, on the first Sunday in March.

with children of all ages.

Three of the main ski resorts – Bansko, Borovets and Pamporovo – have specialist children's ski schools that organise snow crèches, children's races and other competitions. Bansko is the favourite resort of families as it offers other, non-skiing activities such as ice skating and sleigh rides.

There are many things for children to do in and around Sofia, from ceramic painting on the ground floor of TZUM to Sofia Zoo, which has large, open areas for children to explore in safety. Although the Sofia Land amusement park is currently closed due to security issues, the Puppet Theatre, at 14 ul Gurko (www.sofiapuppet. com), will keep children amused, even though all performances are in Bulgarian. There is a children's swimming pool at the Hotel Princess, and all the major hotels organise Sunday brunches with entertainment for children.

Bulgarians in general love children and will go out of their way to accommodate them. The main problem with children is keeping them amused while travelling from place to place, as roads are poor and trains slow, meaning that travelling times can be long.

Food should not be a problem, as Bulgarians themselves are not fond of spicy foods, while universal children's favourites, such as omelettes, or steak with chips, are found on every menu in the country.

CALENDAR OF FESTIVALS

Many festivals in Bulgaria follow the old, Julian calendar, in which Easter usually falls a week or two after the Western Easter.

January/February New Year's Day, known as St Vassal's (St Basil's) Day, is celebrated in the Pernik and Dupnitsa regions with Kukeri festivals. Some parts of the country still celebrate Christmas Day according to the old calendar, on 6 January.

March Kukeri festival at Shiroka Luka, first Sunday in March.

April Orthodox Easter is best celebrated at the Alexander Nevski Cathedral in Sofia or at Rila Monastery.

May Varna International Pop Festival takes place during the last week of May; the International Biennale of Humour and Satire is held in Gabrovo in odd-numbered years. The Koprovshtitsa Folklore Festival straddles May and June.

June The Festival of the Roses takes place in Kazanlak during the first weekend of June; Varna International Music and Theatre Festival is held every year towards the end of the month.

July Verdi Festival held in Plovdiv during the first week of July.

August Folk festivals in Bourgas and Varna; the Festival of the Sea in Balchik and Sozopol; the Dunov Festival in the Rila lakes; the Pirin Song Festival. The dates are not fixed. The Rozhen Sings festival takes place during the last week of August; the Bagpipe Festival at Mugla is held on the last Sunday of August. Assumption Day (15 August) is celebrated with ritual processions at any church that has a temporal connection with the Virgin Mary.

September The Krustova Gora Festival of the Cross takes place on 14 September, celebrated in Bulgaria as Day of the Cross; the Apollonia Arts Festival in Sozopol, with performances of opera, classical music and theatre, is held on the causeway.

October St John of Rila day at Rila Monastery; wine harvest festival in Melnik (both on 18 October).

December Kukeri festivals on Christmas Day in Blagoevgrad. New Year's Eve celebrations and fireworks in Sofia and elsewhere.

EATING OUT

Eating well is not going to be a problem in Bulgaria. The country's cuisine – a mix of Balkan, Turkish and Slavic influences – can appear meat-heavy at first, but on closer inspection it's tasty, great value and healthy. Much importance is placed on the use of local ingredients, and a new generation of inventive young chefs is taking Bulgarian food to new places, often via modern twists of classic dishes. Even the smallest towns have at least one good restaurant, usually more, and service – notoriously bad until quite recently – has improved hugely. Prices remain cheap, although those who do want to splurge will find ample opportunity, particularly in Sofia.

Vegetarians, long neglected, will have little problem finding a wide range of dishes, not least as the practice of observing Orthodox Lent – frowned on during the communist period – once again has many adherents. There are four periods of the year (not to mention every Wednesday and Friday) when the faithful refrain from eating meat, fish and dairy products, and restaurants have adapted menus to cater to this group.

Café in Nessebar

Bulgarians tend to eat light breakfasts of sweet coffee with bread and yoghurt, followed by an early lunch of considerable proportions: at least two courses. Evening meals are taken late, around 8pm or even later. The main Easter meal is eaten after midnight mass on Saturday night. Such meals, especially in large families, can often go on all night.

LOCAL INGREDIENTS

The quality of pork *(svinsko)* is of the highest order throughout the Balkans, and Bulgaria is no exception. One of the main staples, it appears in any number of dishes. Chicken and veal are also popular and most other meats are readily available. Beef tends to be expensive and not always of the best quality.

Though Bulgaria has a not insignificant coastline, fish is not as available as it should be. Carp, trout and perch are the most popular local fish served in restaurants, and are usually grilled. Nessebur has the coast's best selection of seafood restaurants. All along the coast you will find street vendors selling *tsatsi*, small, sardine-like fish fried in a rudimentary batter and covered in salt. They taste great. Black Sea mussels are small yet tasty, cheap and enormously popular.

Given the fact that Bulgarians claim to have invented yoghurt, known locally as *kiselo mlyako*, they make no bones about adding it, even if only a small amount, to almost any dish. If you are unsure about whether your food will come with yoghurt, ask: *Mozhe li da prigotvite yastieto bes kiselo mlyako?* Can you make this dish without yoghurt?

Bulgarian fruit and vegetables are of excellent quality, though strictly seasonal. Agriculture is slowly adopting Western techniques and practices, but most produce remains organic, and as a result tastes superb. Tomatoes especially have a flavour that long ago disappeared from the supermarkets of western Europe. Sweetcorn is popular in season (August and early September) and you will find street vendors selling boiled cobs all over the country. Melons, both water and honeydew, are fabulous and appear at the end of July. Prices are high at the beginning of the season, but by the end of September they are all but given away.

Bulgarian bread, which accompanies virtually every dish, is usually dusted with oil and served hot.

POPULAR DISHES

Defining what is actually Bulgarian national cuisine, as opposed to what is merely Balkan, is difficult. Dishes that the Bulgarians claim as their own, such as *shkembe chorba* (tripe soup) or *kashkaval pane* (fried, breaded cheese) for instance, are just as likely to be found in Macedonia, Romania, Serbia and even Turkey. There are, of course, local variations that go beyond differences in spelling, and pure Bulgarian dishes include *sirene po shopski* (baked goat's cheese) and *kavarma* (meat and vegetable stew, often very spicy). Other popular dishes include *tarator* (a thick cold yoghurt and cucumber soup, often served as a starter), *kiopolou* (roasted or grilled aubergines and peppers, often served covered in

Local ingredients at a festival in Sofia

Kavarma (meat and vegetable stew)

vinegar), *kiuftete* (meat balls, either pork or chicken, usually flattened out to look like hamburger patties), *chuski biurek* (fried or baked peppers stuffed with beans and cheese) and *giuvech* (a thick stew usually served in the pot it was cooked in, and a staple of all Bulgarian-cuisine restaurants).

When it comes to snacks, Bulgarians love savouries: you will see *gevrek* (a kind of bagel topped with salt) and *banitsa* (a light pastry filled with cheese) sold everywhere; they are best eaten piping hot. *Semki* (sunflower seeds) are eaten as though they were the last food in the world. Go to a football match in Bulgaria and by the end of the game you will be knee-deep in sunflower seed shells.

You will find that Bulgarian desserts tend to consist of very sweet Turkish derivatives, such as *baklava* or *revane*. *Halvitsa*, a kind of nougat, is also popular, but it is rarely found in restaurants. Ice-cream sellers litter the country's streets all summer long.

WHERE TO EAT

There are now a large number of Bulgarian restaurants, known as *mehana*, where traditional dishes are served, often accompanied by a folklore show of variable taste and quality. Choice is usually limited in these establishments, however, and you may often hear the phrase *Za sezhalenie ... svershi* (We do not have...).

Though you should try Bulgaria's main dishes, at some stage you may want something a little more familiar. The Black Sea coast is full of dubious establishments with such names as London Pub or Wembley Pride, all serving the standard English fried breakfast and roast beef lunches. Sofia has some fine international restaurants, including the

☉ YOGHURT

Bulgarians invented yoghurt, or so they will tell you. Certainly, people in the region have made yoghurt throughout history to preserve milk, much in the same way as Northern Europeans have made cheese and butter. The earliest yoghurts were probably spontaneously fermented, perhaps by wild bacteria residing inside goatskin bags used for transport. It was originally produced exclusively on a domestic scale, using sheep's milk. The word for yoghurt comes from the Turkish verb *yogurtmak* (to blend), but its active ingredient is called *Lactobacillus bulgaricus*, a fact that only supports the Bulgarian claim to have invented it.

Yoghurt remains a staple of the Bulgarian diet. It is often taken at breakfast, though it can be eaten, or drunk, at any time throughout the day. It is also used as an ingredient in many Bulgarian dishes, the most popular of which is the cold soup *tarator*.

now legendary Japanese restaurant at the Marinela Hotel. Chinese food is also popular among Bulgarians and you will find Chinese restaurants all over the country, even in the most remote towns. Finding a good Indian meal is impossible outside of Sofia.

WHAT TO DRINK

Wine

Grape cultivation and wine production in Bulgaria dates back to antiquity. The Pomorie region has been known for wine since the Thracians planted the first vines around 1500 BC. Today grapes for wine are grown in most parts of the country and exported to Europe, the US, Japan and China. The state-owned vineyards have nearly all been privatised, and quality has rocketed, though to give the devil his due, the Communist state's monopoly Vinprom invested heavily in Australian and American machinery and know-how in the 1970s and 1980s, which laid the foundation for the excellent wines produced today.

> ### Side dishes
>
> When eating out, especially in traditional Bulgarian restaurants, make sure you ask the waiter if the dish you have ordered will be accompanied by a *garnitura* (side dish). It is usual in this country to order and pay for everything separately, including bread.

There are five main wine regions: Eastern, Northern, Sub-Balkan, Southern and South-Western. The best white wine tends to come from the Eastern region, as the warmth and moisture of the coastal air add fruitiness to the grapes. The leading labels of the region are Jambol and Stambolovo.

Harvesting grapes in Plovdiv

Red wines are the speciality of the Northern region and the vineyards around Ruse on the Danubian plain. Use of the noble Cabernet Sauvignon, which is especially suited to the cooler, damper soil and long warm autumns, is common, though local varieties of grape are also used. The leading wineries are those at Ruse, Suhindol and Ljaskovets.

The other regions are less noted, with a couple of exceptions. The Sungulare Misket and Sungulare Eau de Vie are whites of abundant flavour from the depths of the Balkan valleys, while perhaps the most famous Bulgarian wine, the fruity white Misket of the Valley of the Roses, is produced in the Sub-Balkan region. The most famous winery in the country is that in Assenovgrad, which produces the Mavrud and Gamza reds.

You will find a good selection of wines at all super-markets throughout the country, though there are also a number of specialist wine merchants in Sofia, Plovdiv, Rousse, Varna and Bourgas. Purchasing wine direct from a winery tends not to be any cheaper than doing so from ordinary shops, and you are likely to be limited to the wines bottled at the vineyard.

Spirits

The local spirit is *rakia*, made of prunes or grapes, often at home. You can buy *rakia* in supermarkets, but the home-brewed stuff is best. It is often drunk as an aperitif, and if you are invited to a Bulgarian home you will simply not be able to escape trying it. Do not resist; embrace its charms. The taste is something that can be acquired afterwards. Another popular local drink is *boza*, a thick, slightly alcoholic and rather sickly brown juice made from wheat, barley or switch grass.

Beer

This is produced in abundance and is much more popular with local people than wine. Most breweries are owned by major international companies and quality is always high. The leading local brands are Boliarka from Veliko Tarnovo, Astika from Haskovo and Zagorka from Stara Zagora. Boliarka also produces a bizarre stout called Stolichno. Beer is almost always bought in bottles, even in pubs, and

Rakia, a spirit made from prunes or grapes

pubs selling draught beers are rare, even in Sofia. Imported beers are widely available but expensive.

TO HELP YOU ORDER...

Can I see the menu? **Izvinete munyuto, molya?**

I'm a vegetarian. **Az sum vegetarianets.**

Can I have a beer, please? **Edna bira, molya.**

Please may I have the bill. **Smetkata, molya.**

Water choice

Bulgarian tap water is safe to drink, but the huge number of springs dotted throughout the country make bottled water so cheap that almost the entire population eschews the tap.

MENU READER

beef **govezhdo**
beer **bira**
boiled potatoes **vereni kartofi**
bread **khlyap**
carp **sharan**
cheese **sirene**
chicken **pileshko**
chips (French fries) **perzheni kartofi**
coffee **kafe**
eggs **yaitsa**
fish **riba**
honey **met**
juice **sok**
kebab **kebap**
lamb **agneshko**

mackerel **skumriya**
mashed potatoes **kartofeno piuray**
meatball **kiufte**
milk **mlyako**
mineral water **mineralna voda**
pork **svinsko**
rice **oris**
salad **salata**
salmon **syomga**
sausages **karnache**
schnitzel **shnitzel**
steak **biftek**
tea **chay**
trout **pestarva**
wine **vino**

PLACES TO EAT

We have used the following symbols to give an idea of the price per head for a three-course meal for one, including wine:

€€€€	more than 50 leva
€€€	25–50 leva
€€	10–25 leva
€	under 10 leva

SOFIA

Aubergine €€€ *11 ul Carnegie, tel: (88) 999 18 67.* Bulgarian food with a modern twist served in a small house with a lovely, colourful courtyard in good weather. The ever-changing menu is short yet everything on it is a notch above the Sofia average. Usually has at least two excellent beef dishes.

Bai Gencho €€ *15 ul Dondulkov, tel: (02) 986 65 50.* As famous for its wine collection as its food, Bai Gencho – a traditional Bulgarian restaurant – is easy to find on Dondulkov, a short walk towards the opera from TZUM. Five shops of the same name sell a great range of wines at various locations around Sofia.

Boyansko Hanche €€€ *1 pl Sborishte, Boyana, tel: (89) 859 29 06.* Up in the hills close to the Boyana church, this place serves big portions of classic Bulgarian dishes in a gorgeous setting. Traditional décor and occasional live music can give it a touristy feel, but locals love the place too.

Egur, Egur €€ *10 ul Dobrudzha, tel: (02) 989 33 83.* Armenian food, superbly prepared, presented and served in a legendary restaurant owned by Bulgarian-Armenian jazz singer Hilda Kazasyan. Loads of vegetarian options, and a sublime wine cellar. Reservations essential.

Halbite €€ *72 ul Neofit Rilski, tel: (88) 780 40 65.* Serves a wide variety of beers from around Bulgaria alongside a decent range of local and international food. Lots of grilled meat and a wider than usual vegetarian selection. Nice beer garden.

Made In Home €€€ *30A ul Angel Kanchev, tel: (87) 688 40 14.* Exactly what the name suggests: homemade, organic food served in a quirky setting reminiscent of a cosy country kitchen. Seafood is a speciality, not least the Black Sea mussels and prawns. A small place – you may need a reservation.

Moma €€€€ *28 ul Solunska, tel: (88) 562 20 20.* Not cheap – in fact it costs a fortune to eat here – but this is one of Sofia's greatest ever restaurants. Chic, inventive, even playful food is prepared by a top kitchen team never afraid to try out new things. Delicious slow-cooked lamb.

Pri Miro €€€ *34 ul Murphy, tel: (02) 943 71 27.* Bulgaria's top Serbian restaurant, owned and run by the eponymous Miro, who usually cooks everything too. Great *cevapcici*, *pleskavice* and the tangiest *ajvar* (Serbian relish) in the land. Not to be missed; advance reservations essential.

Pod Lipite €€ *1 ul Elin Pelin, tel: (02) 866 50 53.* Bulgarian artists and writers have been eating in this charming house opposite the Borisova garden since the 1920s. The food is centered on slow-cooked, oven-baked meat dishes but has a good vegetarian menu and a great wine list.

Rainbow Factory € *10 ul Veslets, tel: (02) 444 05 56.* Good value pitstop destination. Salads, pastries, tortillas, sandwiches, great coffee and always the coolest music playing over the speakers. The young, friendly staff do their best to meet the huge demand at lunchtime.

Seasons €€€€ *1 bul Bulgaria (Hilton Sofia), tel: (02) 933 50 62.* Few Hilton hotels in the world have a restaurant to match Seasons in the consistently high quality of its food. For those who can afford the prices, a visit will be a highlight of any stay in Sofia. International and Bulgarian dishes rub shoulders on an interesting menu.

Secret €€€ *12 bul Tsar Osvoboditel, tel: (87) 844 44 74.* Probably the best place in the capital to sample new Bulgarian food, a mix of the tradi-

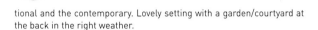

tional and the contemporary. Lovely setting with a garden/courtyard at the back in the right weather.

Street Chefs €€ *58–60 ul Parchevich*. No more than a food truck parked in a courtyard with a few tables, this is nevertheless where to come for Sofia's best gourmet burger. Enormously popular during the summer the queues speak for themselves. The fries are as good as the burgers.

The Studio €€€€ *4 pl Narodno Sobranie (Radisson Blu Sofia), tel: (02) 933 43 34*. Perhaps the finest dining in Sofia, the Radisson Blu's flagship diner offers those with the deepest pockets an ever-changing menu of inventive, Modern European dishes based around seasonal ingredients. Fine wines and the city's best selection of cigars do not help those trying to keep the bill down.

Supa Star € *8 ul Tsar Ivan Shishman*. There are salads and sandwiches on the menu at this cheap, colourful place popular with students but as the name suggest the real draw is the great soup, all made daily on the premises. There are always at least seven or eight varieties to choose from.

AROUND THE COUNTRY
Bansko

Most of Bansko's hotels and guesthouses have on-site *mehanas* – local restaurants – almost all of which are good. The best is the one at Hotel Bansko at 17 ul Glazne.

Baryakova Mehana €€ *3 ul Velyan Ognev, tel: (0749) 844 82*. Legendary *mehana* in the heart of Bansko's Old Town that comes into its own during the winter when open fires and cheap-as-you-like, huge portions of local dishes are served to local people and tourists enjoying the accompanying music.

Come Prima €€€€ *98 ul Pirin (Kempinski Grand Arena), tel: (0749) 888 88*. If the *mehanas* of Bansko get too much, try this small, exquisite restaurant at the Kempinski. Decorated in imperial, turn-of-the-19th-century style, the ever-changing menu gives you a culinary tour of the Mediterranean.

Dedo Pene €€ *ul Bujnov, tel: (0749) 883 48,* www.dedopene.com. Probably Bansko's best-known restaurant, this place is located in the town centre in a traditional building dating from 1820, and offers a boisterous Bansko experience to the tour groups who flock here – which means it is often crowded. Small hotel upstairs.

Obetsanovata Kushta €€€ *pl Vazrazhdane, tel: (0749) 822 36.* Perhaps the oldest *mehana* in Bansko, this place will happily serve you an entire pig on a spit if you give 48 hours notice. There are simple grilled meats and local dishes available for the less adventurous.

Voyvodata Mehana € *58 ul Pirin, tel: (0888) 894 284.* A huge range of meat and fish dishes, as well as great service make this place a first choice for many returning visitors to Bansko. The garden is a delight in good weather, the cellar rather charming in colder months.

Plovdiv

Alafrangite €€ *17 ul Kiril Nektariev, tel: (032) 26 95 95.* Delightful restaurant set in a beautiful National Revival-period house in Old Plovdiv. Well-prepared and presented traditional Bulgarian meals served by staff who really appear to care. Chamber music is played in the lovely courtyard most evenings during the summer.

Odeon €€ *40 ul Otets Paisiy, tel: (088) 797 68 90.* Food this good should not be this cheap. Inventive, modern European cuisine cooked and served in a charming setting (it has a lovely covered terrace) just a few minutes walk from the city centre.

Puldin €€€ *3 ul Knjaz Tsereletev, tel: (032) 63 17 20.* The best and most historic restaurant in Plovdiv (and probably the most expensive) is located in the heart of the Old Town. Recently renovated, it retains its original charm. Local dishes predominate: try the *chuksa banitsa* (peppers stuffed with feta cheese), a real treat. Or you can try the Puldin salad, a showcase platter featuring a number of Bulgarian salads. You can eat outside in the garden in the summer.

Smokini €€€ *12 ul Otets Paisiy, tel: (999) 000 996.* The pick of Plovdiv's smart set. Good food served in a highly contemporary setting. The first-floor terrace is a major attraction during the summer: you will need a reservation. There is also a garden, and the wine list is fabulous.

Veliko Tarnovo

Izvora Taverna €€€ *Arbanasi, tel: (062) 60 12 05.* Located close to the Village Museum of Arbanasi, this is one of the best traditional restaurants in the country. It offers just about every Bulgarian dish imaginable, all served by staff in traditional dress, in a garden complete with fountains and ponds, and playgrounds for children. The excellent barbecued lamb dishes are particularly recommended.

Mehana Gurko €€ *33 ul Gurko, tel: (062) 62 78 38.* The best of Veliko Tarnovo's *mehanas* is often full with coach parties, so make sure you reserve a table beforehand. It's all genuine, home-cooked Bulgarian cuisine, though you may have a devil of a time finding the place, on a tiny side street off ul Rakovski. It's worth the hunt, though.

Shtastliveca €€ *79 ul Stefan Stambolov, tel: (062) 60 06 56.* Offering splendid views of the river and lower city, the tables on the terrace and by the window at Shtastliveca are unsurprisingly much sought-after. If you can't bag one, it is still more than worth your while, as the food – mainly Italian – is the best in the city.

THE COAST
Nessebur

Andromeda €€ *ul Ivan Alexander, tel: (0554) 42 079.* Enjoy the fish and the views at this good-value restaurant in Old Nessebur. Impeccably prepared seafood that is a world away from what you will find in the many tourist traps that litter the area.

Plakamoto € *8 ul Ivan Alexander, tel: (088) 880 72 39*. A Nessebur legend, this family-run restaurant serves huge plates of steaming mussels and other treats from the sea all served with stunning sea views. Prices are amazingly low given the location and quality, and the house wine is a drinkable bargain.

White Rose €€ *40 ul Rakovski, tel: (089) 792 52 56*. In the new part of Nessebur, this place is hugely popular and given the standard of the food it is easy to see why. Seafood dominates, but there are plenty of other things to choose from, including vegetarian dishes. The contemporary décor makes a nice change from the more traditional hostelries on the peninsula.

Varna

Godzila €€ *37 bul Maria Luiza, tel: (052) 61 29 05*. A bizarre name for any restaurant, let alone a pizzeria. Rest assured though, the pizza here is the best on the coast: thin and crispy with generous toppings. Look for the Godzilla statue outside.

Kashtata €€ *9 ul 8-mi Noemvri, tel: (052) 60 59 09*. A hidden gem in the old Greek district of Varna. Serves a good choice of Bulgarian food, including a fine selection of charcoal-grilled meats and fish barbecued outside in the garden.

Marche €€€ *Primorski Park, tel: (088) 475 40 75*. Located in the middle of Varna's seafront park, just past the zoo, there is no monkey business here: just outstanding food in a classy setting. French dishes and fine wines take the headlines, but there is pizza too.

Balchik

Dabolka € *Kavarna, tel: (087) 891 13 77*. One of the most famous restaurants in the country. Found on the sea shore at the bottom of a steep hill, Dabolka serves enormous plates of fresh mussels, all farmed right here. Incredibly cheap, no reservations are taken, and you may have to queue at busy times. It's worth the wait.

A–Z TRAVEL TIPS

A SUMMARY OF PRACTICAL INFORMATION

A

ACCOMMODATION

Almost every town, city and resort has a wide choice of accommodation. The Black Sea coast and ski resorts offer the widest range, though Sofia, which has a number of five-star establishments, is catching up fast. In other cities you may be hard pushed to find top-class hotels, but there is always somewhere comfortable and fairly luxurious on offer. Even the lowliest bed-and-breakfast will offer satellite or cable television, and internet access is also standard. Note that hotels on the Black Sea and in ski resorts are much cheaper if booked online in advance. During the peak beach and ski season many places will insist on a minimum stay, usually three nights.

I'd like a... **Bi iskal...**   with a bath **sbanya**
single room **edinichna staya**   with a shower **sdush**
double room **dvoina staya**
What's the rate per day? **Kolko struva stayata?**
I have a reservation. **Rezerviral sem staya.**
Do you have any vacancies? **Imate li svobodna staya?**

AIRPORTS

Sofia, Plovdiv, Varna and Bourgas have international airports. **Sofia**'s airport (Code SOF) – the country's largest and busiest – is a modern, efficient facility. Baggage usually arrives promptly and the only queues – which can be long at peak times – are at passport control. Metro line M2 runs to the city centre from Terminal 2. Tickets cost 1.60 leva and the journey takes 20 minutes. Yellow, metered taxis wait outside and should cover the 15km (10-mile) journey to the town centre for around 20 leva. **Plovdiv** (Code PDV) is served by an airport 12km (7 miles) southeast of the city. Taxi is the only viable option for getting into the city as buses are irregular. Expect to pay 10–15 leva.

Varna (Code VAR) is Bulgaria's best airport, usually served by two flights a day from the capital as well as numerous flights from abroad during the summer. It is some way from the city centre, but cheap taxis abound; the fare to the centre is about 20 leva.

Bourgas airport (Code BOJ) is 12km (7 miles) from the city centre. Bus No. 15 stops outside and runs to the city's main bus station every 30 minutes. Tickets cost 1 leva and can be bought direct from the driver.

> I need a taxi at the airport. **Iskam taksi v letishte.**
> How much? **Kolko?**
> That's too much! **Mnogo e skarpo!**
> Does this bus go to... **Tozi li e avtobusart za...?**

B

BICYCLE HIRE

Almost unheard of a decade ago, cycling is now huge in Bulgaria. In mountain resorts, such as Vitosha/Aleko, Bansko, Pamporovo and Borovets, you can hire mountain bikes at all major hotels for around 20 leva a day, leaving a credit card as deposit. Big hotels in main Black Sea resorts also hire bicycles. See www.motoroads.com/bulgaria-motor cycle-rental-bike-rent.html to hire a motorbike.

BUDGETING FOR YOUR TRIP

Still remarkably cheap by Western standards, prices in Bulgaria are nevertheless increasing fast.

Transport. A standard cross-city taxi ride should not cost more than 20 leva, while bus tickets cost 1 leva in most cities. A one-way flight from Sofia to Varna costs 100–150 leva depending on the day of departure and time of the year.

Eating out. Good cheap cuisine is not hard to find, but in Sofia and on the coast especially, you can easily spend a fortune. A top-class dinner in one of Sofia's five-star hotels will cost at least 100 leva per head, but a standard Bulgarian restaurant off Boulevard Vitosha will serve hearty portions of local fare for under 10 leva per head.

Museums and attractions. You need to pay for entry to all Bulgaria's museums, but prices are incredibly cheap. In smaller towns and cities, you can usually purchase one ticket valid for entry to all museums and galleries.

C

CAR HIRE

To get the best out of Bulgaria, hiring a car for a day or two is essential, but it is relatively expensive, with daily rates starting at around 120 leva. Petrol is cheap, though. All the major companies have offices throughout the country, including Sofia, Plovdiv, Bourgas and Varna airports, and cars can be hired at most big hotels. You need to be 18 to drive a car in Bulgaria, but few hire companies will rent to anyone under 21. You will need a credit card. Many secondary roads are in poor condition; driving at night can be hazardous (see page 119).

Avis Sofia Airport Terminal 2, tel: (02) 945 92 24, www.avis.bg
Europcar Sofia Airport Terminal 2, tel: (02) 2 981 46 26, www.europcar.bg
Hertz 53A bul. Nikolai Vapstarov, Sofia, tel: (02) 439 02 22, www.hertz.bg
Sixt Sofia Airport Terminal 1, tel: (02) 816 95 75, www.sixtbulgaria.com

CLIMATE

In general, Bulgaria's winters are bitterly cold, while summers range from warm to very hot. Spring and autumn tend to be very short and very wet. There are many regional variations. Along the Black Sea coast, winters are more moderate than in Sofia, and summer temperatures can reach Mediterranean heights. The mountains receive large amounts of snow, which may remain until June in some areas. The Danube plain is the country's driest region. The average January temperature range in Sofia is -4–2°C (25–36°F) and July temperatures range from 16–27°C

(61–81°F). Along the Black Sea, average January temperature range is -1–6°C (30–43°F); July temperatures range from 19–30°C (66–86°F).

CLOTHING

Expect rain at any time of year. Bulgarians have few hang-ups about clothing, but note that most local women cover their heads before entering churches and cathedrals; visitors are under no obligation to do the same, however. If invited into a Bulgarian home you should remove – or at least offer to remove – your footwear.

CRIME AND SAFETY

Bulgaria is a safe country. Beggars can be pushy in major tourist areas, especially in Sofia around the Grand Balkan Hotel and TZUM department store, but they are rarely aggressive. Keep your valuables safe, however, especially on public transport. Tram routes to and from Sofia station are notorious for pickpockets, as are buses on the coast. The Black Sea's busiest beaches are also a haven for thieves. Stray dogs carrying rabies pose a threat to travellers in many cities. Call 166 for the police, 150 for an ambulance.

> Where is the police station? **Kade e naybliskiyat politseyski uchastek?**
> My ... has been stolen. **Otkradnaha mi...**
> passport/handbag/wallet **passport/chantata/portfela.**
> Stop thief! **Spri! Krazhba!**
> Help! **Pomisht!**

D

DISABLED TRAVELLERS

Bulgaria is making giant strides towards better accommodating disabled travellers, but getting around remains difficult. Sofia is leading the way, installing rudimentary wheelchair ramps in many public squares, museums, tourist attractions and metro stations. The Black Sea coast is rich in hotels that can accommodate disabled guests. The mountain resorts and other cities are less accessible.

DRIVING

Bulgarians drive on the right, though in the countryside such rules are often seen as being loose, at best. If you bring your car to Bulgaria make sure you have your national driving licence and proof of international insurance cover (a green card). Those who forget can buy insurance at the border. You need to buy a road tax vignette at the border: the cost is €8 per week. Otherwise there are no tolls on any Bulgarian roads.

Driving in major cities is no better or worse than in any other country, but things are very different outside the cities. There are only a couple of motorways: from Sofia to Bourgas and the Turkish border, Sofia to Blagoevgrad and Varna to Shumen. Most other inter-urban roads are single-lane and often packed with lorries. Progress can be slow. Roads in general are poorly signposted, so bring a good map or GPS device. Road surfaces can be poor off main roads, and few highways have lights, so be careful at night. Be wary of random horse-drawn carts and stray animals when passing through villages. The speed limit is 50kmh (31mph) in cities, 90kmh (56mph) on the open road, 130kmh (81mph) on the motorways. Winter tyres are compulsory from November to March. If you should breakdown, call 146.

petrol/diesel **benzin/dizel**
Full tank, please. **Napelnete dogore, molya.**
My car has broken down. **Stana avariya.**
There's been an accident. **Stana katastrofa.**
Can I park here? **Moga li da ostavya kolata si tuk?**

E

ELECTRICITY

200 volts AC. Visitors from the US will need an adaptor.

EMBASSIES AND CONSULATES

Australia (consulate): 37 ul Trakia, Sofia, tel: (02) 946 13 34.
Canada 7 ul Volga, Sofia, tel: (02) 969 97 10.
South Africa 7 ul Shipka, Sofia, tel: (02) 983 35 05.
UK 9 ul Moskovska, Sofia, tel: (02) 933 92 22.
US 16 ul Kozyak, tel: (02) 937 51 00.

EMERGENCIES

Ambulance/Police/Fire Brigade: **112** or Ambulance **150**, Police **166**, Fire Brigade **160**.

Fire! **Pozhar!**
Help! **Pomisht!**
Call the... **Molya, povikayte...**
police/ambulance/fire brigade **politsiya/lineyka/
pozharnata**
I want to contact my embassy. **Iskam da napravia vruska
smoeto posolstvo.**

G

GETTING THERE

Served by a wide variety of airlines, Bulgaria is cheap and easy to reach. Flying remains the quickest way, but romantics may like to take the train, and an improving road infrastructure means driving to and from Bulgaria is not the arduous activity it once was.

By air. The country is dotted with airports, of which the busiest are Sofia, Plovdiv, Varna and Bourgas. All are served by scheduled flights from most European capitals, operated by a wide variety of airlines, from national flag carrier Bulgaria Air (www.air.bg) to low-cost airlines Easy Jet, Ryan Air and Wizz Air. Prices are cheap if you book well in advance. Note that most flights to Varna and Bourgas are seasonal, operating in summer only. In winter, scheduled flights are supplemented by charters to Plovdiv (serving the ski resorts). There are currently no direct flights from the US.

By train. You can enter Bulgaria by train from Romania (at Ruse from Bucharest); from Greece (at Kulata, from Athens and Salonika); from Turkey (at Kapitan Andreevo, from Istanbul). There is also a daily train to Sofia from Budapest that runs via Belgrade.

By road. There are numerous land crossings into Bulgaria from Romania, Turkey, Greece, Macedonia and Serbia. The busiest, and those most likely to be used by western visitors, are at Ruse (from Romania), Kapitan Andreevo (from Turkey), Kulata and Makaza (from Greece) and Kalotina (from Serbia-Montenegro). Borders can be very busy during the summer, especially those crossing into Greece. You should always allow plenty of time and expect delays.

H

HEALTH AND MEDICAL CARE

There are no specific health risks, but you should take out adequate health insurance cover or have a valid EHIC before departing. General standards of health care are fine. In an emergency call **112 or 150** for an ambulance. Emergency medical treatment is free, but you may have to pay for some medicines, and you should tip the doctor and nurses. If you want private medical care, head for **IMC Medical** in Sofia, at 28 ul Gogol, tel: (02) 944 93 26. Tap water is safe to drink, though the low cost of the bottled variety means that very few people actually do. Mosquitoes are a problem all over the country during summer, so insect repellent is essential. Stray dogs can be a problem in many cities; bites are more common in summer than winter. Though outbreaks of rabies are rare, should you be bitten, go to a hospital immediately for a rabies injection. Pharmacies are ubiquitous: look out for green crosses. Most stay open late, many 24 hours, even in smaller towns.

> chemist **apteka**
> dentist **zubolekar**
> doctor **lekar**
> I need a doctor who speaks English. **Iskam lekar s angliyski ezik.**

L

LANGUAGE

Bulgarian is a Slavic language, closely related to Serbian, Croatian and Slovene, and resembles Russian due to its use of the Cyrillic script, which can appear impenetrable to the visitor. We advise you to spend an hour or two learning the Cyrillic characters, as few signs – even in Sofia and on the coast – appear in Latin script, and knowledge of the alphabet will save both time and stress. To assist with navigation, we have included the Cyrillic for main locations in the Where to Go chapter.

English is widely spoken along the Black Sea coast and in the ski resorts, less so in urban areas (even Sofia) and not at all in the countryside. German will get you further, while Russian, though spoken to an extent by most Bulgarians of a certain age, is met with derision.

> **The Bulgarian Cyrillic alphabet**
> А   а   **a** as in **a**nnual
> Б   б   **b** as in **b**ill

В	в	**v** as in **v**ictory
Г	г	**g** as in **g**lory
Д	д	**d** as in **d**esert
Е	е	**e** as in **e**nd
Ж	ж	**zh** as in plea**s**ure
З	з	**z** as in **j**azz
И	и	**i** as in **i**nn
Й	й	**y** as in oka**y**
К	к	**k** as in **k**ing
Л	л	**l** as in **l**og
М	м	**m** as in **m**iss
Н	н	**n** as in **n**oun
О	о	**a** as in b**a**ll
П	п	**p** as in **p**olice
Р	р	**r** as in **r**ival
С	с	**s** as in **S**weden
Т	т	**t** as in **t**oday
У	у	**u** as in p**u**t
Ф	ф	**f** as in **f**oot
Х	х	**h** as in **h**olland
Ч	ч	**ch** as in **ch**elsea
Ц	ц	**ts** as in **ts**ar
Ш	ш	**sh** as in **sh**ow
Щ	щ	**sht** – like sh from **sh**ow with t from **t**oday
Ъ	ъ	**a** as in **a**bout
ь	ь	**y** as in can**y**on
Ю	ю	**you** as in **you**th
Я	я	**ya** as in **ya**hoo

Double sounds

ий		**i** as in like **ea**st
оо		**o** as in like c**oo**peration
дж		**dzh** as in **j**am, **j**ob

Some useful words
yes/no **da/ne**
please **molya**
thank you **mersi**
excuse me **izvinete me**
good morning **dobro utro**
good afternoon **dobar dan**
good night **dobar vecher**
goodbye **dovizdhanay**

Days of the week
Monday **ponedelnik**
Tuesday **vtornik**
Wednesday **sryada**
Thursday **chetvurtek**
Friday **petak**
Saturday **sobota**
Sunday **nedelya**

Numbers
one **edin**
two **dva**
three **tri**
four **chetiri**
five **pet**
six **shest**
seven **sedem**
eight **osem**
nine **devet**
ten **deset**
eleven **edinayset**
twelve **dvanayset**
thirteen **trinayset**
fourteen **chetirinayset**
fifteen **petnayset**
sixteen **shestnayset**
seventeen **sedemnayset**
eighteen **osemnayset**
nineteen **devetnayset**
twenty **dvayset**
twenty-one **dvayset i edin**
twenty-two **dvayset i dva**
twenty-three **dvayset i tri**
thirty **triyset**
forty **chetiriyset**
fifty **pedeset**
sixty **shestdeset**
seventy **sedemdeset**
eighty **osemdest**
ninety **devetdeset**
one hundred **sto**
one thousand **hilyada**

LGBTQ

Same-sex sexual activity has in practice been legal in Bulgaria since 1968. However, although attitudes towards members of the LGBTQ community are changing slowly, civil partnerships and same-sex marriages are still not recognised. There is a small gay scene in Sofia but travellers should beware of making any public shows of same-sex affection.

M

MAPS

Most hotel concierges will be able to provide you with a free city or town map, usually with a guide to the city's sights. The best country map, produced by Kartografiya Eood, can be found at most international travel bookshops. This company also produces excellent maps to the Pirin, Rila and Balkan mountain ranges, with routes and cabins well marked. These are essential for serious hiking trips.

MEDIA

In Sofia and Plovdiv, the English-language listings magazine *In Your Pocket* is a useful free resource: find it in most hotels and at tourist information offices. There are no English-language newspapers, but the excellent website Novinite (The News; www.novinite.com) provides Bulgarian news in English, including weather and travel information, and is updated several times per day. Most hotels and apartments offer BBC News, CNN and Euronews as part of their TV packages.

MONEY

Bulgaria's currency is the lev, plural leva. Banknotes come in denominations of 100, 50, 20, 10, 5, 2 and 1. You will also find 1 and 2 leva coins. The lev is divided into 100 *stotinki*, which come in denominations of 50, 20, 10, 5, 2 and 1.

Many services, especially taxis, can unofficially be paid for in euros – notes only, and do not expect change.

Changing money or traveller's cheques is best done inside a bank. Never change money on the street. ATMs are ubiquitous, and Visa/MasterCard credit cards are accepted in hotels, restaurants and shops. American Express and Diners Club cards are less welcome.

> Where is the nearest bank? **Znaete li kade tuk ima banka?**
> I want to change... **Iskam da smenya...**
> some money **liri**
> some traveller's cheques **tozi patnicheski chek**
> The ATM has swallowed my card **Bankomatet ne vrushta kartata mi**

O

OPENING HOURS

Government offices and banks open Mon–Fri 8.30am–3pm, later in bigger cities. Museum hours vary but are often 10am–6pm. Most museums close on Monday, some on Sunday and, particularly in the countryside, they close for lunch. Shops and supermarkets open Mon–Sat 9am–6pm, but many stay open later, and most shops in Sofia open on Sunday.

P

POLICE

Police are usually helpful and friendly, though in most cases do not speak English. The police force shows little interest in foreign tourists, so unless you go looking for trouble or decide to drive at excessive speeds, you will have little to do with them. Should you need them in an emergency, shout loudly or dial 112.

Where's the police station? **Kade e nay bliskiyat politseyski uchastek?**
I've lost my... **Zagubi si...**
passport/luggage **pasport/bagash**

POST OFFICES

Post offices can be found in most cities and towns, though if you are posting something abroad, it is best to do it from Sofia or Varna, or else your intended recipient could be waiting for some time. The central post office in Sofia is at 6 ul Gurko, behind the Radisson Hotel, and is open Mon–Sat 7.30am–8pm. In Varna the main post office is at 36 bul Saborni, opposite the Cathedral of the Assumption, and is open Mon–Fri 7.30am–8pm, Sat 7.30am–1pm. Post boxes are yellow and have a trumpet painted on them.

For urgent letters and packets DHL have offices in most major cities (open Mon–Sat). Call 0700 17 700 for DHL in Sofia.

I want to send this by... **Molya, tova pismo da bede...**
airmail **svezdushna poshta**
express **serza poshta**

PUBLIC HOLIDAYS

The biggest public holiday is Easter. The date of Orthodox Easter, set using the old Julian calendar, usually falls a week or more after Catholic and Protestant Easter, and sometimes after 1 May. Only Easter Sunday and Monday are considered holidays. Good Friday is a normal working day. Unlike in the UK, if a holiday falls on a weekend, the next working day is not substituted.

1 January New Year's Day

April/May Orthodox Easter
1 May Labour Day
3 May Liberation Day
6 May Army Day
24 May Education Day (in honour of Sts Cyril and Methodius)
6 September Reunion Day
22 September Independence Day
24, 25, 26 December Christmas

For more details on local religious and other festivals, see page 98.

R

RELIGION

The vast majority of the Bulgarian population is Eastern Orthodox, similar in most ways to the Orthodoxy practised in Russia, Romania, Serbia, Montenegro and Macedonia, though somewhat different from (and frequently at odds with) Greek Orthodoxy. There are also Muslim, Jewish and Catholic minorities – around 700,000 ethnic Turks remain in Bulgaria, and around 5,000 Jews.

T

TELEPHONES

The country code for Bulgaria is +359. The city code for Sofia is 02, and for Varna 052. Other important city codes include: Blagoevgrad 073, Bourgas 056, Plovdiv 032, Veliko Tarnovo 062. However, many telephone operators now have their own codes. In all cases, the first 0 in the city code is dropped when making an international call to Bulgaria. When dialling within Bulgaria the city code is used in. To dial out of Bulgaria, dial 00, the country and city code, then the number. You can dial internationally from most hotel rooms (at an extravagant cost). Public phones require a phonecard, available from newsstands and kiosks.

Bulgaria is well covered by four mobile phone networks, and only the most remote areas suffer from a lack of coverage. EU citizens who have roaming enabled you will be able to use their phones as at home.

TIME DIFFERENCES

Bulgaria is two hours ahead of Greenwich Mean Time. Like the UK, it uses daylight saving time in summer. The chart below shows the times in Sofia and various other cities.

New York	London	Jo'burg	**Sofia**	Sydney	Auckland
5am	10am	noon	**noon**	9pm	11pm

TIPPING

You should tip restaurant staff (but check your bill to ensure that service is not already included), domestic hotel staff and doormen. In these cases a 10 percent tip is seen as obligatory, regardless of whether you have been happy with the service. Taxi drivers do not expect to be tipped, and you should do so only if you have taken a particularly short journey, in order to make the ride worth the driver's time and trouble. Tip all health staff.

TOILETS

There are few decent public toilets in Bulgaria. In Sofia the only ones we would recommend are in the city's shopping malls and the basement of the Halite. In the mountains even restaurant and mountain retreat toilets may leave a lot to be desired, and many are of the common squat variety. You should bring your own toilet paper.

Where are the toilets? **Kadye e toaletnata?**

TOURIST INFORMATION

Though Bulgaria no longer has an established tourist information office network abroad but has instead developed a good internal network of tourist information offices. Most towns and cities now have some kind of information office. Bulgaria's excellent official tourist information website is www.bulgariatravel.org.

Bansko: pl Nikola Vapstarov 1, tel: (0749) 88 580
Plovdiv: pl Tsentralen 1, tel: (032) 62 02 29
Sofia: 1 pl Sv Nedelya, tel: (02) 933 58 26
Varna: pl Sveti Sveti Kiril I Metodiy, tel: (052) 82 06 90
Veliko Tarnovo: 5 ul. Hristo Botev, tel: (088) 765 98 29

> tourist information office **touristicheska informaciya**
> Do you have a map of Sofia? **Imate li karta na Sofia?**
> Are there any tours of the city? **Provezhdat li se obikolki iz grada?**

TRANSPORT

Taxis. Taxis in Bulgaria were once unregulated rip-offs. Now, thanks to legislation, all are metered, must provide all clients with a receipt, and in Sofia at least all have to be yellow. That is not to say that visitors are never fooled into paying too much; some are. But if you keep your wits about you and always use a taxi that clearly displays the name of the company it belongs to (Yellow Taxi 02-911 19; EuroTaxi 02-910 33; Sofia Taxi 02-974 47 47; OK Supertrans 02-973 21 21 in Sofia) you will find taxis astonishingly cheap. Don't expect drivers to speak English,

> Take me to this address. **Kam [address], molya.**
> Please stop here. **Mozhe li da sprete tuk?**

however, and you may like to ask your hotel concierge or restaurant waiter to order one for you.

Trains. The railway network is extensive, cheap and generally reliable, though somewhat slow. Even the optimistically named *InterCity* and *Expres* trains are gruelling. The quickest of the five daily trains from Sofia to Varna takes almost eight and a half hours. If you do wish to travel cross-country by train, it is best to do so at night, on a sleeper (*spalen*), which offers good value and allows you to pass the hours unconscious. Buying tickets can be a laborious process; expect no help from ticket staff. Fortunately, the Bulgarian Railways website (www.bdz.bg/en) is very good and most tickets can now be bought online, at least 24 hours in advance.

> How much is the fare to...? **Kolko shte struva do...?**
> I want a ticket to... **Iskam edin bilet za...**
> single (one way) **ednoposochen bilet**
> return (round trip) **dvuposochen bilet**
> first/second class **perva klasa/ftora klasa**

Aeroplanes. Bulgaria has three internal air routes, between Sofia, Varna and Bourgas, operated by both the national carrier Bulgaria Air and Wizz Air. Tickets for domestic routes sell for around 120–150 leva each way, but can be even cheaper if booked far enough In advance.

V

VISAS AND ENTRY REQUIREMENTS

Citizens of the EU and EEA countries (Switzerland, Norway, Iceland) may enter Bulgaria visa-free. Americans, Australians, Canadians and New Zealanders may enter visa-free, but are limited to stays of 30 days. Passports must be valid for at least three months after entry.

Citizens of almost all other countries, including South Africa, need a visa from a Bulgarian Embassy abroad before travelling – they cannot be purchased at the border. For a list of Bulgarian consulates and visa requirements, visit the Bulgarian Foreign Ministry's website (www.mfa.bg).

Customs regulations are standard, and duty-free allowances follow international norms: two bottles of alcohol, 200 cigarettes or 50 cigars or 25g of tobacco are personal limits. Bulgaria belongs to the EU so there are no limits for those travelling to and from EU countries. Cash in excess of €10,000 must be declared on entry.

W

WEBSITES AND INTERNET ACCESS

www.bulgariatravel.org/en Bulgaria's official tourism website
www.novinite.com English-language Bulgarian news website
www.inyourpocket.com Free guides and smartphone apps for a number of Bulgarian cities
www.bzn.bg/en Bulgarian railways, complete with timetables and on-line ticket sales
www.visitsofia.bg/en Official tourism website for the capital Sofia
www.visitplovdiv.bg/en Plovdiv's excellent official website
visit.varna.bg/en Event listings for Varna and much of the Bulgarian coastal resorts

Y

YOUTH HOSTELS

Bulgaria is packed with good, cheap hostels, all offering beds in shared dorms for around 20 leva or even less. Most offer private rooms for 10 leva or so more. The best places get busy in high season and booking is advised. Both www.hostelbookers.com and www.hostelworld.com have a wide selection to choose from.

RECOMMENDED HOTELS

A wide variety of good, cheap accommodation has long been one of Bulgaria's best assets as a tourist destination. Bargain hunters will never have to look far for a decent room at a fair price, while those looking to spend a little more on high-end luxury will likewise not be disappointed: the selection of first-class hotels both in the cities and the beach resorts is the equal of anywhere in the world. It is worth noting, however, that whatever level of accommodation you choose, it pays to book well in advance. The ski and beach resorts in particular are often fully booked during high season, and if you turn up on spec you will pay far more than people on package tours. To arrange accommodation in advance www.bgstay.com is a good resource, as is www.booking.com. A huge number of private apartments and villas have been built in the main ski and seaside resorts in recent years, and were mainly sold to foreign investors who let them out on a weekly basis. These can often be a good-value option, especially for families and large groups. The websites www.holidaylettings.co.uk and www.airbnb.com list thousands of Bulgarian holiday homes for rent.

€€€   **more than 200 leva**
€€   **100–200 leva**
€   **under 100 leva**

SOFIA

Art'Otel €€ *44 ul William Gladstone, tel: (02) 980 60 00*, www.artotel.biz. Stylish hotel just off bul Vitosha. Just 19 elegant rooms, all individually decorated and offering good-value accommodation. The Tower Suite is the best.

Arena di Serdica €€€ *2–4 ul Budapeshta, tel: (02) 810 77 77*, www.arenadiserdica.com. When the foundations were dug, the remains of a Roman amphitheatre were found, and the hotel built around the ruins. The results are spectacular and make the Arena unique. This is genuine modern luxury in the most ancient of settings.

Grand Hotel Sofia €€€ *1 ul Gurko, tel: (02) 811 08 11*, www.grandhotelsofia. bg. Opposite the National Theatre, this outstanding hotel is classy from beginning to end. Smartly dressed doormen welcome you in, friendly reception staff meet and greet you, while the sheer opulence of the spacious rooms will ensure your stay is a pleasurable and luxurious one.

Hilton Sofia €€€ *1 bul Bulgaria, tel: (02) 933 50 00*, www.hilton.com. This homage to glass was built in 2000 and is well positioned next to the National Palace of Culture (NDK). Even the standard rooms are large, let alone the executive rooms and suites. Excellent restaurant. This is one of the best Hiltons there is.

Holiday Inn Sofia €€ *111 bul Alexandar Malinov, tel: (02) 807 07 07*, www. holidayinn-bg.com. Although the location in the Sofia business park is not the best for tourists, the quality is high and prices are surprisingly low, especially at weekends when the conference crowd is absent. There's a huge swimming pool and fitness centre. A good choice for those with their own car.

Marinela €€€ *100 bul James Bourchier, tel: (02) 969 22 22*, www.hotel-marinela.com. Now a Sofia icon, the Marinela was built in the 1970s by a Japanese businessman and designed by a renowned Japanese architect. Boasting large rooms with exquisite views, the Japanese garden is a highlight, and the hotel is home to the city's best Japanese restaurant.

Meg-Lozenetz €€ *84 ul Krum Popov, tel: (02) 965 19 70*, www.meg-lozenetz. com. Newish three-star hotel offering good-value, tasteful rooms. In a nice, residential area close to the National Palace of Culture (NDK).

Radisson Blu €€€ *4 pl Narodno Sabranie, tel: (02) 933 4334*, www.radisson blu.com. This shining glass edifice is close to Alexander Nevski Cathedral. Fine, luxurious rooms and five-star service. Has a superb health and fitness centre, and offers superb in-house dining options.

Renaissance €€ *2 pl Vazrazhdane, tel: (02) 986 0939*, www.hotel-renaissance-bg.com. Delightful over-the-top decoration complete with Renaissance-era reproductions at every turn make this an enjoyable place to stay. Large, good-value rooms and a sublime roof terrace.

Sofia Hotel Balkan €€€ *5 pl Sveta Nedelya, tel: (02) 981 64 51,* www.sofia balkan.com. The oldest of the city's five-star hotels and still the number one choice of travellers for whom location is everything. A living piece of the city's history, the Sofia Balkan stands imposingly on Sofia's central square and offers all the amenities and luxury you would expect from one of Europe's great hotels.

Art Hostel € *21A ul Angel Kanchev, tel: (02) 987 05 45,* www.art-hostel. com. Delightful, well-priced bed and breakfast establishment on the same site as one of Sofia's best hostels. Some (but not all) rooms have private bathrooms: be sure to check when booking. Great breakfast included in the price.

Sofia Plaza €€ *154 bul Hristo Botev, tel: (02) 813 7912,* www.hotelsofia plaza.com. Comfortable, reasonably priced accommodation close to Sofia's main railway station. Rooms are on the small side of cosy, but are well equipped and brightly decorated.

AROUND THE COUNTRY
Bansko

Avalon € *4 ul El tepe, tel: (0749) 88 399,* www.avalonhotel-bulgaria.com. A terrific family-owned and -run hotel on a quiet residential street close to the city centre. The rooms on the top floor are the best, with the sloping ceilings and mountain views providing bags of character.

Chateau Vaptsarov €€ *23 ul Solun, tel: (0700) 12 622,* www.chateau vaptzarov.com The stunning Chateau has large, comfortable rooms (although not as luxurious as the exterior may suggest), plus a large health complex with sauna, steam bath, hot tub and massage. Price includes daily transport to the gondola lift.

Evelina Palace €€ *98 ul Ikonom Chuchulain 34, tel: (087) 819 60 43,* www.eve linapalace.com. Large bright rooms and a wonderful swimming pool, complete with separate children's area, make this attractive hotel a hit with families. Staff are the friendliest in town and the buffet breakfast is superb.

Kempinski Grand Arena €€€ *ul Pirin, tel: (0749) 888 88,* www.kempinski-bansko.com. Next to the gondola lift, the location of this huge, luxurious hotel could not be better. Nor could the service, staff, rooms or restaurants. Set over five interconnected buildings, this is one of the few Bansko hotels that have genuinely tried to blend with their mountainous surroundings. The spa and wellness centre, with a huge indoor pool, will keep non-skiers occupied.

Pirin €€€ *bul Tsar Simeon, tel: (0749) 981 13 86,* www.hotelpirin.com. This historic hotel close to Bansko's central square is one of the best in the resort. Indoor swimming pool, fitness centre, sauna, solarium, steam room and excellent *mehana*.

Borovets

Note that in Borovets and Pamporovo the streets have no name.

Ice Angels €€ *tel: (075) 032 045,* www.iceangelshotel.com. Located quite literally on the slopes, Ice Angels offers big rooms, amazing views and a superb buffet breakfast. Rooms usually sell out months in advance.

Rila €€€ *tel: (0750) 326 58,* www.rilaborovets.com. For many years the monolithic Rila Hotel *was* Borovets, and it remains very much a resort within a resort. Recently extended, it now has a glorious indoor swimming pool with mountain views, fitness centre and kindergarten. Rooms are large but spartan.

Vila Stresov €€€ *tel: (02) 980 42 92 (Sofia office),* www.villastresov.com. Stunning, Swiss-style villa in a lovely setting. Rooms are luxurious, and there is a sauna, jacuzzi and leafy garden. The best accommodation in Borovets, it comes at a price.

Yastrabets €€€ *tel: (0750) 322 12,* www.hotelyastrebets.bg. One of the most luxurious hotels in the resort, complete with huge wellness centre. It is located at the foot of the Yastrabets ski runs, close to the gondola lift. The terrace here is the resort's most popular – when the weather is good enough to use it.

Pamporovo

Extreme €€ *tel: (0879) 933 308*, www.hotel-extreme.bg. Despite the name, you do not have to be an extreme snowboarder to stay at this elegant contemporary hotel. Rooms are large, the restaurant is very good and the bar is one of the resort's liveliest. There is après-ski massage and relaxation in an onsite spa centre too.

Finlandia €€ *tel: (030) 218 367*, www.hotelfinlandia.com. Looking as Scandinavian as the name suggests, the interiors of the Finlandia may be a little dated but it is a comfortable and great value option. It is a bit of trek to the slopes, but there is a free shuttle bus.

Malina Village € *tel: (088) 813 70 07*, www.malina-pamporovo.com. Cosy two-level chalets in a quiet part of the resort offer a back-to-nature way to enjoy Pamporovo. Most chalets have en-suite saunas, and the village has a restaurant.

Mourgavets €€ *tel: (0309) 58 190*, www.murgavets-bg.com. Ugly as hell but as comfortable as heaven, the Mourgavets is as plush on the inside as it is brutal on the out. Offers terrific views from its upper floors and is very good value for money.

Mursalitsa €€ *tel: (0309) 540 00*, www.mursalitsa.com. Closer to the slopes than most Pamporovo hotels, the Mursalitsa offers a variety of comfortable rooms. Nice communual areas, complete with a lounge with log fire during winter.

Plovdiv

Coco Guest House €€ *32 ul. Hristo Dyukmedzhiev, tel: (087) 880 1883*, www.coco-plovdiv.com. Small boutique guest house in the heart of The Trap – Plovdiv's trendy cultural hub. Classically furnished rooms come with all mod cons. Staff are incredibly helpful and friendly.

Noviz €€ *55 bul Ruski, tel: (032) 63 12 81*, www.novizhotel.com. Small but reasonably smart, if old-fashioned, four-star hotel opposite Budjarnik

Park. All bathrooms have a tub – a definite plus in this part of the world – and prices include a good breakfast in the hotel restaurant.

Grand Hotel Plovdiv €€€ *2 ul Zlatyu Boyadzhiev, tel: (032) 93 44 44,* www. grandhotelplovdiv.bg. Situated on the northern bank of the Maritsa River, this sparkling five-star is Plovdiv's best hotel. Overlooking the gorgeous slopes of the Rhodopes, it is close to the trade fair grounds and is often full during May and September. Reservations are essential.

Odeon € *40 ul. Otets Paisiy, tel: (032) 622 065,* www.hotelodeon.net. Gorgeous little place in the heart of the old town. Rooms are small and yet wonderfully furnished with bags of character, from the plush carpets to the wooden-beamed ceilings. The hotel restaurant is one of the city's best.

Ramada Trimontium €€€ *2 ul Kapitan Raicho, tel: (032) 60 50 00,* www. trimontium-princess.com. This grand, classically designed hotel dominates pl Tsentralen. The hotel casino is a favourite with visiting businessmen. The rooms are enormous, and recent renovation has returned them to former glories.

Veliko Tarnovo

Arbanassi Palace €€€ *Arbanasi, tel: (062) 630 176,* www.arbanassi palace.bg. Luxurious and understandably expensive hotel on a small side road leading from the village-museum of Arbanasi, a 10-minute drive from Veliko Tarnovo. The bathrooms are bigger than most Bulgarian apartments, and the view from the terrace towards Veliko Tarnovo is nothing short of wondrous. From riding school to Roman bath – everything you could ever wish for is here.

Premier €€ *1 ul Sava Penev, tel: (062) 61 55 55,* www.hotel-premier-bg.com. The best hotel in Veliko Tarnovo itself, with rooms offering great views of the valley and the rest of the town. All rooms have internet access and large bathrooms. Two rooms are fitted out for use by travellers with disabilities.

Tsarevets €€ *23 ul Chitalishtna, tel: (062) 60 18 85,* www.hoteltsarevets.com. This is a delightful hotel, situated on a quiet street in the heart of old Veliko

Tarnovo. Originally a merchant's house, built in 1891, it has been completely refurbished, yet all the rooms remain elegantly and classically furnished. The high ceilings are wonderful, as are the views from almost all the rooms.

Yantra Grand €€ *2 ul Opalchenska, tel: (062) 60 06 07,* www.yantrabg. com. Centrally located with views of the mountains and – in some cases – the Tsarevets Fortress, the Yantra combines modern amenities with decent service in a classical building. There is a casino for high rollers next door, operated by the same people.

THE COAST

Nessebur

Arsena Beach €€ *Yujen Plaj, tel: (0554) 46 610,* www.mpmhotels.bg. Elegant hotel on Nessebur's South Beach (Yujen Plaj). The modern, chic interiors provide a stark contrast to the Old Town, visible across the water from the balconies of most rooms.

Marieta Palace €€ *45 ul Lyuben Karavelov, tel: (0554) 44 111,* www.marieta palace.com. Looking not unlike a huge cruise ship, the hotel is in the commercial heart of Nessebur. Futuristic in design, it has fantastic swimming pools and a wide range of comfortable rooms.

Nessebur Royal Palace €€ *19 ul Mitropolitska, tel: (0554) 46 490,* www. nessebarpalace.com. In the heart of the Old Town, next to two historic churches, this hotel perfectly blends the old and the new. Rooms are large and classically furnished, the bathrooms quite remarkable. Terrific restaurant on site.

St Nikola € *2 ul Kraibrejna, tel: (0554) 46 686,* www.hotel-st-nikola.com. Good, simple and very well-priced accommodation on the northern side of the Old Town, with views towards Sunny Beach. Staff are friendly and helpful. Note that breakfast is not included in the price.

St Stefan €€ *11 ul Ribarska, tel: (0554) 43 603,* www.hotelsaintstefan. com. The best-value hotel in the Old Town. It blends perfectly with the ancient surroundings, and besides big, comfortable rooms has a good fish restaurant and lovely garden.

Balchik

Antik €€ *16 ul Primorska, tel: (0888) 205 020,* www.hotelantik.eu. The Black Sea coast's best kept secret: a smart little family-run hotel offering great-value rooms on the seafront: most rooms have balconies looking out to sea. Superb terrace serving outstanding seafood.

Thracian Cliffs €€€ *Bozhurets, Kavarna, tel: (057) 092 200,* www.thracian cliffs.com. Luxury hotel complete with championship golf course on the Kavarna peninsula, just north of Balchik. Besides amazing rooms with superb views, the hotel has its own private beach.

Varna

Aqua €€ *12 ul Devnya, tel: (052) 63 90 90,* www.aquahotels.com. This large, modern hotel opposite the railway station is popular with tour groups, and in high season it can often be fully booked. The suites are great value. Reservations recommended.

Capitol €€€ *40 ul Petko Karavelov, tel: (052) 68 80 00,* www.capitol.bg. Probably the classiest hotel in Varna itself, the Capitol offers large, stylish rooms and a splendid restaurant in a location close to the entrance of the municipal beach.

Grand Hotel Varna €€€ *St Elias Complex, Sv Konstantin, tel: (052) 36 14 91,* www.grandhotelvarna.com. The best hotel on the coast is actually outside Varna, in the satellite resort of Sv Konstantin, a 10-minute drive from the city centre. Every luxury is on offer in the 296 rooms and 35 suites. There are indoor and outdoor pools and the beach is a short walk away.

Panorama €€€ *bul Primorski 31, tel: (052) 68 73 00,* www.panoramabg.com. In an enviable location at the end of Varna's main promenade, with magnificent views out to sea, this is central Varna's top hotel, and is priced accordingly. Plenty of free extras, including underground parking.

DICTIONARY

adj adjective   **adv** adverb   **BE** British English   **n** noun   **prep** preposition   **v** verb

A

accept *v* приемам *priyemam*, съгласявам се *saglasyavam se*

access *n* достъп *dostap*

accident *n* злополука *zlopoluka*, нещастен случай *neshtasten sluchay*

accommodation настаняване *nastanyavane*

account *n* (**bank**) сметка *smetka*

acupuncture акупунктура *akupunktura*

adapter адаптер *adapter*

address *n* адрес *adres*

admission (price) такса за вход *taksa za vhod* (цена *tsena*)

after *adv* след *sled*; **~noon** следобед *sledobed*; **~shave** след бръснене *sled brasnene*

age *n* възраст *vazrast*

agency агенция *agentsiya*

AIDS СПИН *spin*

air *n* въздух *vazduh*; **~ conditioning** климатик *klimatik*; **~-dry** изсушавам на въздух *izsushavam na vazduh*; **~ pump** въздушна помпа *vaz-*

dushna pompa; **~line** авиолиния *avyoliniya*; **~mail** въздушна поща *vazdushna poshta*; **~plane** самолет *samolet*; **~port** летище *letishte*

aisle коридор *koridor*; **~ seat** място до коридора *myasto do koridora*

allergic алергичен *alergichen*; **~ reaction** алергична реакция *alergichna reaktsiya*

allow разрешавам *razreshavam*

alone сам *sam*

alter *v* сменям *smenyam*

alternate route алтернативен път *alternativen pat*

aluminum foil алуминиево фолио *aluminievo folyo*

amazing изумителен *izumitelen*

ambulance линейка *lineyka*

American *adj* американски *amerikanski*

amusement park увеселителен парк *uveselitelen park*

anemic анемичен *anemichen*

anesthesia упойка *upoyka*

animal животно *zhivotno*

ankle глезен *glezen*

antibiotic *n* антибиотик *antibiotik*

antiques store антиквариат *antikvariyat*

antiseptic cream антисептичен крем *antiseptichen krem*

apartment апартамент *apartament*

appendix (body part) апендикс *apendiks*

appetizer предястие *predyastie*

appointment среща *sreshta*

arcade аркада *arkada* (arch.), пасаж *pasazh*

area code пощенски код *poshtenski kod*

arm *n* (**body part**) рамо *ramo*

aromatherapy ароматерапия *aromaterapiya*

around (the corner) наблизо *nablizo*; **~ (price)** приблизително *priblizitelno*

arrival пристигане *pristigane*

arrive пристигам *pristigam*

artery артерия *arteriya* (**blood transportation**), магистрала *magistrala* (**Road**)

arthritis артрит *artrit*

art изкуство *izkustvo*

Asian *adj* азиатски *azyatski*

aspirin аспирин *aspirin*

asthmatic астматичен *astmatichen*

ATM банкомат *banko-mat*; **~ card** банкова карта *bankova karta*

attack *v* атакувам *atakuvam*

attraction (place) атракция *atraktsiya*

attractive привлекателен *privlekatelen*

Australia Австралия *avstralya*

Australian *adj* австралийски *avstraliyski*

automatic автоматичен *avtomatichen*; **~ car** кола с автоматична скоростна кутия *kola s avtomatichna skorostna kutiya*, кола-автомат *kola avtomat*

available достъпен *dostapen*

B

baby бебе *bebe*;
~ **bottle** бебешка
бутилка *bebeshka
butilka*; ~ **wipe**
мокра кърпичка
mokra karpichka;
~**sitter** детегледачка
detegledachka

back (body part) гръб
grab; ~**ache** болка в
гърба *bolka v garba*;
~**pack** раница *ranitsa*

bag чанта *chanta*,
торбичка *torbichka*

baggage (BE) багаж
bagazh; ~ **claim**
получаване на багаж
poluchavane na bagazh;
~ **ticket** багажен
етикет **(label)** *baga-
zhen etiket*, багажен
билет **(paid luggage)**
bagazhen bilet

bake v пека *peka*

bakery фурна *furna*,
пекарна *pekarna*

ballet балет *balet*

bandage превръзка
prevrazka, бинт *bint*

bank n банка *banka*

bar (place) бар *bar*

barbecue (device) n
грил *gril*

barber фризьор *frizyor*

baseball бейзбол
beyzbol

basket (grocery store)
кошница *koshnitsa*

basketball баскетбол
basketbol

bathroom баня *banya*

battery батерия *bateriya*

battleground бойно
поле *boyno pole*

be v съм *sam*

beach плаж *plazh*

beautiful ; ~ красив
krasiv

bed n легло *leglo*;
~ **and breakfast**
нощувка със закуска
noshtuvka s zakuska

before преди *predi*

begin започвам
zapochvam

beginner начинаещ
nachinaesht

behind (direction)
отзад *otzad*

beige adj бежов *bezhof*

belt колан *kolan*

best adj най-добър
naydobar; ~ **before**
най-добър до
naydobar do

better по-добре
podobre

bicycle колело *kolelo*

big голям *golyam*; ~**ger**
по-голям *pogolyam*

bike route
велосипедна пътека
velosipedna pateka

bikini бикини *bikini*

bill n **(money)**
банкнота *banknota*;
~ n **(of sale)** сметка
smetka, квитанция
kvitantsiya

bird птица *ptitsa*

birthday рожден ден
rozhden den

black adj черен *cheren*

bladder мехур *mehur*

bland любезен
lyoubezen

blanket одеяло *odeyalo*

bleed кърви *karvya*

blender блендер
blendar

blood кръв *krav*;

~ **pressure** кръвно
налягане *kravno
nalyagane*

blouse блуза *bluza*

blue adj син *sin*

board v борд *bord*;
~**ing pass** бордна
карта *bordna karta*

boat n лодка *lodka*,
кораб *korab*

boil v варя *varya*

bone n кост *kost*

book n книга *kniga*;
~**store** книжарница
knizharnitsa

boot n ботуш *botush*

boring скучен *skuchen*

botanical garden
ботаническа градина
botanicheska gradina

bother v безпокоя
bezpokoya

bottle n бутилка
butilka; ~ **opener**
отварачка *otvarachka*

bowl n чаша *chasha*,
купа *kupa*

boxing match боксов
мач *boksov mach*

boy момче *momche*;
~**friend** приятел
priyatel

bra сутиен *sutyen*

bracelet гривна *grivna*

brake (car) спирачка
spirachka

breaded паниран
paniran

break v **(bone)** чупя
chupya

breakdown (car)
повреда *povreda*

breakfast n закуска
zakuska

break-in (burglary) n
обир *obir*, кражба

чрез взлом *krazhba
chrez vzlom*

breast гръд *grad*; ~**feed**
v кърмя *karmya*

breathe дишам *disham*

bridge мост *most*

briefs (clothing)
пликче *plikche* **(for
ladies)**, слипове
slipove

bring нося *nosya*

British adj английски
angliyski

broken adj **(bone)**
счупен *schupen*

brooch брошка *broshka*

broom метла *metla*

brother брат *brat*

brown adj кафяв *kafyav*

bug (insect) n бръмбар
brambar

building сграда *sgrada*

burn v горя *gorya*,
изгарям *izgaryam*

bus авто*avtobus*;
~ **station** автогара *avtogara*; ~ **stop** спирка
spirka; ~ **ticket**
автобусен билет
avtobusen bilet; ~ **tour**
автобусна обиколка
avtobusna obikolka

business adj служебен
sluzheben; ~ **card**
визитка *vizitka*;
~ **center** бизнес
център *biznes tsentar*;
~ **class** бизнес класа
biznes klasa; ~ **hours**
работно време *rabotno
vreme*

butcher n касапин
kasapin

buttocks задник *zadnik*

buy v купувам *kupuvam*

bye чао *chao*

C

cabaret кабаре *kabare*

cable car кабинков лифт *kabinkov lift* **(transportation line in the mountains)**, кабинка на лифт *kabinka na lift* **(one vagon of the mountain lift)**

cafe (place) кафене *kafene*

call v **(phone)** телефонирам *telefoniram*; ~ n - **collect** разговор за сметка на приемащия *razgovor za smetka na priyemashtya*

calorie калория *kaloriya*

camera фотоапарат *fotoaparat*; ~ **case** калъф за фотоапарат *kalav za fotoaparat*; **digital** ~ цифров фотоапарат *tsifrov fotoaparat*

camp v къмпингувам *kampinguvam*; **~ing stove** печка за къмпинг *pechka za kamping*; **~site** къмпинг *kamping*

can opener отварачка за консерви *otvarachka za konservi*

Canada Канада *kanada*

Canadian adj канадски *kanadski*

cancel анулирам *anuliram*

candy бонбон *bonbon*

canned good консервиран продукт *konserviran produkt*

canyon каньон *kanyon*

car кола *kola*; ~ **hire** **[BE]** коли под наем *koli pod naem*; ~ **park** **[BE]** паркинг *parking*; ~ **rental** рент-а-кар *rent a kar*, коли под наем *koli pod naem*; ~ **seat** автомобилна седалка *avtomobilna sedalka*

carafe кана *kana*

card n карта *karta*; **ATM** ~ банкова карта *bankova karta*; **credit** ~ кредитна карта *kreditna karta*; **debit** ~ дебитна карта *debitna karta*; **phone** ~ телефонна карта *telefonna karta*

carry-on n **(piece of hand luggage)** ръчен багаж *rachen bagazh*

cart (grocery store) количка *kolichka*; ~ **(luggage)** количка за багаж *kolichka za bagazh*

carton (of cigarettes) стек (цигари) *stek tsigari*; ~ **(of groceries)** кутия *kutiya*, кашон *kashon*

cash n пари в брой *pari v broy*; ~ v обръщам в пари в брой *obrashtam v pari v broy*

cashier касиер *kasyer*

casino казино *kazino*

castle замък *zamak*

cathedral катедра *katedra*

cave n пещера *peshtera*

CD CD *sidi*

cell phone мобилен телефон *mobilen telefon*

Celsius Целзий *tselziy*

centimeter сантиметър *santimetar*

certificate сертификат *sertifikat*

chair n стол *stol*; ~ **lift** седалков лифт *sedalkov lift*

change v **(baby)** сменям пелена *smenyam pelena*; ~ **(buses)** прекачвам се *prekachvam se*; ~ **(money)** обменям пари *obmenyam pari*; ~ n **(money)** обмен на валута *obmen na valuta*

charge v **(credit card)** плащам с кредитна карта *plashtam s kreditna karta*; ~ **(cost)** плащане, разход *plashtane, razhod*

cheap евтин *evtin*; **~er** по-евтин *poevtin*

check v **(luggage)** регистрирам *registriram*; ~ **(in something)** проверявам *proveryavam*; n **(payment)** чек *chek*; **~-in** регистрирам се *registriram se* **(verb)**, чекиране *chekirane* **(noun)**; **~ing account** разплащателна сметка *razplashtatelna smetka*; **~-out** напускам *napuskam*

Cheers! На здраве! *na zdrave*

chemical toilet химическа тоалетна *himicheska toaletna*

chemist [BE] аптека *apteka*

chest (body part) гръден кош *graden kosh*; ~ **pain** болка в гръдния кош *bolka v gradnya kosh*

chewing gum дъвка *davka*

child дете *dete*; **~'s seat** детска седалка *detska sedalka*

children's menu детско меню *detsko menyou*

children's portion детска порция *detska portsiya*

Chinese adj китайски *kitayski*

chopsticks пръчици за хранене *prychitsi za hranene*

church църква *tsarkva*

cigar пура *pura*

class n класа *klasa*; **business** ~ бизнес класа *biznes klasa*; **economy** ~ икономична класа *ikonomichna klasa*; **first** ~ първа класа *parva klasa*

classical music класическа музика *klasicheska muzika*

clean v чиста *chistya*; ~ adj **(clothes)** чисто *chisto*; **~ing product** средства за почистване *sredstva za pochistvane*

clear v **(on an ATM)** анулирам *anuliram*

cliff клиф *kliv*

cling film [BE] хранително фолио *hranitelno folyo*

close v (a shop) затварям *zatvaryam*

closed затворено *zatvoreno*

clothing облекло *obleklo*; **~ store** магазин за облекло *magazin za obleklo*

club n клуб *klub*

coat сако *sako*, палто *palto*

coin монета *moneta*

colander решето *resheto*

cold n (sickness) настинка *nastinka*; **~** adj (temperature) студено *studeno*

colleague колега *kolega*

cologne одеколон *odekolon*

color n цвят *tsvyat*

comb n гребен *greben*

come v идвам *idvam*

complaint оплакване *oplakvane*

computer компютър *kompyoutar*

concert концерт *kontsert*; **~ hall** концертна зала *kontsertna zala*

condition (medical) състояние *sastoyanye*

conditioner (hair) балсам *balsam*

condom презерватив *prezervativ*

conference конференция *konferentsiya*

confirm потвърждавам *potvarzhdavam*

congestion (medical) конгестия *kongestiya*

connect (internet) свързвам *svarzvam*

connection (travel/ internet) връзка *vrazka*; **~ flight** трансферен полет *transferen polet*

constipated запек *zapek*

consulate консулство *konsulstvo*

consultant специалист *spetsyalist*

contact v свързвам се с *svarzvam se s*

contact lens контактни лещи *kontaktni leshti*; **~ solution** разтвор за контактни лещи *raztvor za kontaktni leshti*

contagious заразен *zarazen*

convention hall конферетна зала *konferentna zala*

conveyor belt транспортна лента *transportna lenta*

cook v готвя *gotvya*

cool adj (temperature) студен *studen*

copper n мед *med*

corkscrew n тирбушон *tirbushon*

cost v струва *struva*

cotton памук *pamuk*

cough v кашля *kashlya*; **~** n кашлица *kashlitsa*

country code код на държава *kod na darzhava*

cover charge цена на куверт *tsena na kuvert*

cream (ointment) мехлем *mehlem*, крем *krem*

credit card кредитна карта *kreditna karta*

crew neck с кръгла яка *s kragla yaka*

crib детско легло *detsko leglo*

crystal n (glass) кристал *kristal*

cup n чаша *chasha*

currency валута *valuta*; **~ exchange** обмен на валута *obmen na valuta*; **~ exchange office** обменно бюро *obmenno byouro*

current account [BE] текуща сметка *tekushta smetka*

customs митница *mitnitsa*

cut v режа *rezha*; **~** n (injury) рана *rana*

cute симпатичен *simpatichen*

cycling колоездене *koloezdene*

D

damage v повреждам *povrezhdam*

dance v танцувам *tantsuvam*; **~ club** дискотека *diskoteka*; **~ing** ресторант с танци *restorant s tantsi*

dangerous опасен *opasen*

dark adj тъмен *tamen*

date n (calendar) дата *data*

day ден *den*

deaf adj глух *gluh*

debit card дебитна карта *debitna karta*

deck chair шезлонг *shezlong*

declare v (customs) декларирам *deklariram*

decline v (credit card) отказвам *otkazvam*

deep adj дълбок *dalbok*

degree (temperature) градус *gradus*

delay v закъснявам *zakasnyavam*

delete v (computer) изтривам *iztrivam*

delicatessen деликатесен магазин *delikatesen magazin*

delicious вкусен *fkusen*

denim дънков плат *dankov plat*

dentist зъболекар *zabolekar*

denture чене *chene*, изкуствени зъби *izkustveni zabi*

deodorant дезодорант *dezodorant*

department store супермаркет *supermarket*

departure (plane) заминаване *zaminavane*

deposit v (money) депонирам *deponiram*; **~** n (bank) влог *vlog*

desert n пустиня *pustinya*

detergent препарат за почистване *preparat za pochistvane*

develop v (film) проявявам *proyavyavam*

diabetic adj диабетичен *dyabetichen*; n диабетик *dyabetik*

dial v набирам номер *nabiram nomer*

diamond диамант *dyamant*

diaper пелена *pelena*

diarrhea диария *dyarya*

diesel дизелово гориво *dizelovo gorivo*

difficult труден *truden*

digital цифров *tsifrov*; **~ camera** цифров фотоапарат *tsifrov fotoaparat*; **~ photo** цифрова снимка *tsifrova snimka*; **~ print** дигитален печат *digitalen pechat*

dining room трапезария *trapezariya*

dinner вечеря *vecherya*

direction посока *posoka*

dirty мръсен *mrasen*

disabled *adj* (person) инвалид *invalid*; **~ accessible** [BE] достъп за инвалиди *dostap za invalidi*

disconnect (computer) разединявам *razedinyavam*

discount *n* намаление *namalenye*

dishes (kitchen) посуда *posuda* (dishes and pots)

dishwasher съдомиялна *sadomiyalna*

dishwashing liquid препарат за миене на чинии *preparat za miyene na chinii*

display *n* (device) екран *ekran*; **~ case** витрина *vitrina*

disposable *n* за еднократна употреба *za ednokratna upotreba*; **~ razor** бръсначка *brasnachka*

dive *v* гмуркам се *gmurkam se*

diving equipment оборудване за гмуркане *oborudvane za gmurkane*

divorce *v* развеждам се *razvezhdam se*

dizzy *adj* замаян *zamayan*

doctor *n* лекар *lekar*

doll *n* кукла *kukla*

dollar (US) долар *dolar*

domestic вътрешен *vatreshen*; **~ flight** вътрешен полет *vatreshen polet*

door врата *vrata*

dormitory общежитие *obshtezhitye*

double bed двойно легло *dvoyno leglo*

downtown *n* център *tsentar*

dozen дузина *duzina*

dress (clothing) рокля *roklya*; **~ code** дрескод *dreskod*

drink *v* пия *piya*; **~** *n* питие *pitye*; **~ menu** меню напитки *menyou napitki*; **~ing water** питейна вода *piteyna voda*

drive *v* карам кола *karam kola*

driver's license number номер на шофьорска книжка *nomer na shofyorska knizhka*

drop *n* (medicine) капка *kapka*

drowsiness сънливост *sanlivost*

dry clean химическо чистене *himichesko chistene*; **~er's** химическо чистене *himichesko chistene*

dubbed с дублаж *s dublazh*

during по време на *po vreme na*

duty (tax) мито *mito*; **~-free** безмитно *bezmitno*

DVD DVD *dividi*

E

ear ухо *uho*; **~ache** болка в ухото *bolka v uhoto*

earlier по-рано *po rano*

early рано *rano*

earring обица *obitsa*

east *n* изток *iztok*

easy лесно *lesno*

eat *v* ям *yam*

economy class икономична класа *ikonomichna klasa*

elbow *n* лакът *lakat*

electric outlet електрически контакт *elektricheski kontakt*

elevator асансьор *asansyor*

e-mail *v* изпращам e-mail съобщение *izprashtam imeyl saobshtenye*; **~ e-mail** имейл *imeyl*; **~ address** e-mail адрес *imeyl adres*

emergency спешен случай *speshen sluchay*; **~ exit** авариен изход *avariyen izhod*

empty *v* празен *prazen*

end *v* завършвам *zavarshvam*; **~** *n* край *kray*

engaged (person) сгоден *sgoden*

English *adj* английски *angliyski*; **~** *n* (lan- guage) английски език *angliyski ezik*;

engrave гравирам *graviram*

enjoy изпитвам удоволствие от *izpitvam udovolstvye ot*, харесвам *haresvam*

enter *v* (place) влизам *vlizam*

entertainment развлечение *razvlechenye*

entrance вход *vhod*

envelope плик пощенски *plik poshtenski*

epileptic *adj* епилептичен *epileptichen*; **~** *n* епилептик *epileptik*

equipment оборудване *oborudvane*

escalator ескалатор *eskalator*

e-ticket електронен билет *elektronen bilet*

EU resident резидент на ЕС *rezident na evropeyskya sayuz*

euro евро *evro*

evening *n* вечер *vecher*

excess baggage свръхбагаж *svrahbagazh*

exchange *v* обменям *obmenyam*; **~** *n* (place) обменно бюро *obmenno byouro*; **~ rate** обменен курс *obmenen kurs*

excursion екскурзия *ekskurziya*

excuse *v* извинявам се *izvinyavam se*

exhausted изтощен *iztoshten*

exit v излизам *izlizam*; ~ n изход *izhod*

expensive скъп *skap*

experienced опитен *opiten*

expert експерт *ekspert*, специалист *spetsyalist*

exposure (film) кадър *kadar*, експониране *eksponirane*

express adj -експресен *ekspresen*; ~ **bus** експресен автобус *ekspresen avtobus*; ~ **train** експресен влак *ekspresen vlak*

extension (phone) вътрешен номер *vatreshen nomer*

extra adj допълнителен *dopalnitelen*; ~ **large** много голям *mnogo golyam*

extract v **(tooth)** изваждам *izvazhdam*

eye око *oko*

eyebrow wax восък за вежди *vosak za vezhdi*

F

face n лице *litse*

facial n за лице *za litse*

family n семейство *semeystvo*

fan n **(appliance)** вентилатор *ventilator*

far (distance) далече *daleche*

farm n земеделско стопанство *zemedelsko stopanstvo*, ферма *ferma*

far-sighted далекоглед *dalekogled* (eyes conditons), предвидлив *predvidliv* (predictive)

fast adj бързо *barzo*

fat free обезмаслен *obezmaslen*

father n баща *bashta*

fax v изпращам факс *izprashtam faks*; ~ n факс *faks*; ~ **number** номер на факс *nomer na faks*

fee n такса *taksa*, възнаграждение *vaznagrazhdenye*

feed v храня *hranya*, ям *yam*

ferry n ферибот *feribot*

fever n температура *temperatura*, треска *treska*

field (sports) игрище *igrishte*, стадион *stadyon*

fill v **(car)** зареждам *zarezhdam*

fill out v **(form)** попълвам *popalvam*

filling n **(tooth)** пломба *plomba*

film n **(camera)** фотолента *fotolenta*, фотографска лента *fotogravska lenta*

fine n **(fee for breaking law)** глоба *globa*

finger n пръст *prast*; ~**nail** нокът *nokat*

fire n огън *ogan*; ~ **department** пожарна *pozharna*; ~ **door** огнеупорна врата *ogneuporna vrata*

first adj първи *parvi*; ~ **class** първа класа *parva klasa*

fit v **(clothing)** кройка *kroyka*

fitting room пробна *probna*

fix v **(repair)** ремонтирам *remontiram*

fixed-price menu обедно меню на деня *obedno menyou na denya*

flash photography снимане със светкавица *snimane sas svetkavitsa*

flashlight фенерче *fenerche*

flight n полет *polet*

flip-flops джапанки *dzhapanki*

floor n **(level)** етаж *etazh*

florist цветар *tsvetar*, цветопродавач *tsvetoprodavach*

flower n цвете *tsvete*

folk music фолклорна музика *folklorna muzika*

food храна *hrana*; ~ **pro-cessor** кухненски робот *kuhnenski robot*

foot n крак *krak*

football game [BE] футболна среща *futbolna sreshta*, футболен мач *futbolen mach*

for за *za*

forecast n прогноза *prognoza*

forest n гора *gora*

fork n вилица *vilitsa*

form n **(document)** формуляр *formulyar*

formula (baby) детско сухо мляко *detsko suho mlyako*

fort крепост *krepost*

fountain n фонтан *fontan*

free adj свободен *svoboden*

freelance work работа като фрийлансър *rabota kato friylanser*

freezer хладилник *hladilnik*

fresh свеж *svezh*

friend приятел *priyatel*

frozen food замразена храна *zamrazena hrana*

frying pan тиган *tigan*

full-time adj - –(full time job) на пълно работно време *na palno rabotno vreme*

G

game n игра *igra*

garage n **(parking)** гараж *garazh*; ~ n **(for repairs)** автомобилен сервиз *avtomobilen serviz*

garbage bag чувал за боклук *chuval za bokluk*

gas (car) газ *gas*, бензин *benzin*; ~ **station** бензиностанция *benzinostantsiya*

gate (airport) гейт *geyt*, изход *izhod*

gay adj **(homosexual)** гей *gey*; ~**bar** гей-бар *gey bar*; ~ **club** гей-клуб *gey klub*

gel n **(hair)** гел *gel*

generic drug генерично лекарство *generichno lekarstvo*

German adj немски *nemski*; ~ **(language)** немски език *nemski ezik*

Germany Германия *germaniya*

get off (a train/bus/sub-way) слизам *slizam*

gift n подарък *podarak*; ~ **shop** магазин с подаръци *magazin s podaratsi*

girl момиче *momiche*;
~friend приятелка
priyatelka

give v давам *davam*

glass (drinking) чаша
chasha; **~ (material)**
стъкло *staklo*

glasses очила *ochila*

go v **(somewhere)**
отивам *otivam*

gold n злато *zlato*

golf n голф *golf*;
~ course голф
игрище *golf igrishte*;
~ tournament голф
турнир *golf turnir*

good adj добър (masc.)
dobar, добра (femin.)
dobra; добро (neutr) *dobro* ~ n ; **~afternoon**
добър ден *dobar den*;
~ day добър ден *dobar
den*; **~ evening** добър
вечер *dobar vecher*;
~ morning
утро *dobro utro*; **~bye**
довиждане *dovizhdane*

gram грам *gram*

grandchild внук *vnuk*

grandparents баба и
дядо *baba i dyado*

gray adj сив *siv*

green adj зелен *zelen*

grocery store
хранителен магазин
hranitelen magazin

ground floor партер
parter

groundcloth подложка
за палатка *podlozhka
za palatka*

group n група *grupa*

guide n **(book)**
пътеводител *pat-
evoditel*; **~ n (person)**
екскурзовод *ekskurzo-*

vod; **~ dog** куче водач
kuche vodach

gym n **(place)** фитнес
зала *fitnez zala*

gynecologist
гинеколог *ginekolog*

H

hair коса *kosa*;
~brush четка за
коса *chetka za kosa*;
~cut подстригване
podstrigvane; **~ dryer**
сешоар *seshoar*; **~ sa-
lon** фризьорски салон
frizyorski salon; **~spray**
лак за коса *lak za kosa*;
~style прическа
pricheska; **~ stylist**
фризьор *frizyor*

halal халал *halal*

half adj половин *polovin*;
~ n ; **~hour** половин
час *polovin chas*; **~-kilo**
половин киограм
polovin kilogram

hammer n чук *chuk*

hand n ръка *raka*;
~ luggage ръчен
багаж *rachen bagazh*;
~ wash ръчно пране
rachno prane; **~bag
[BE]** чанта *chanta*

handicapped инвалид
invalid; **~-accessible**
достъпно за инвалиди
dostapno za invalidi

hangover махмурлук
mahmurluk

happy щастлив *shtastliv*

hat шапка *shapka*

have v имам *imam*;
~ sex правя секс
pravya seks

hay fever сенна хрема
senna hrema

head (body part) n
глава *glava*; **~ache**
главоболие *glavobolye*;
~phones слушалки
slushalki

health здраве *zdrave*;
~ food store магазин
за здравословна
храна *magazin za
zdravoslovna hrana*

hearing impaired с
увреден слух *s uvreden
sluh*

heart сърце *sartse*;
~ condition сърдечно
състояние *sardechno
sastoyanye*

heat v топля *toplya*; **~er**
нагревател *nagrevatel*;
~ing [BE] отопление
otoplenye

hectare хектар *hektar*

hello здравейте *zdraveyte*

helmet каска *kaska*

help v помагам *pomagam*;
~ n помощ *pomosht*

here тук *tuk*

hi здравей *zdravey*

high висок *visok*; **~chair**
детско столче с
масичка *detsko stolche
s masichka*; **~lights
(hair)** балеяж *baleyazh*;
~way магистрала
magistrala

hiking boots
туристически обувки
turisticheski obuvki

hill n хълм *halm*

hire [BE] (a car)
наемам *naemam*,
вземам под наем
vzemam pod naem;
~ car [BE] вземам
кола под наем *vzemam
kola pod naem*

hockey хокей *hokey*

holiday [BE] празник
praznik, ваканция
vakantsiya

horsetrack хиподрум
hipodrum

hospital болница
bolnitsa

hostel общежитие
obshtezhitie

hot (spicy) лютив
lyutiv; **~ (tempera-
ture)** горещ *goresht*;
~ spring горещ извор
goresht izvor; **~ water**
гореща вода *goreshta
voda*

hotel хотел *hotel*

hour час *chas*

house n къща
kashta; **~hold
goods** покъщнина
pokashtnina; **~keeping
services** услуги за
почистване *uslugi za
pochistvane*

how как *kak*; **~ much**
колко *kolko*

hug v прегръщам
pregrashtam

hungry гладен *gladen*

hurt v наранявам
naranyavam

husband съпруг *saprug*

I

ibuprofen ибупрофен
ibuprofen

ice n лед *led*; **~ hockey**
хокей на лед *hokey
na led*

icy заледен *zaleden*

identification
идентификация *identi-
fikatsiya*, документи
dokumenti

ill болен *bolen*

in в *v*

include *v* обхващам *obhvashtam*

indoor pool (public) закрит басейн *zakrit baseyn* (обществен *obshtestven*)

inexpensive евтин *evtin*

infected заразен *zarazen*

information (phone) информация *informatsiya*; **~ desk** информационен център *informatsionen tsentar*

insect насекомо *nasekomo*~ **bite** ухапване от насекомо *uhapvane ot nasekomo*; **~ repellent** репелент против насекоми *repelent protiv nasekomi*

insert *v* (card) въвеждам *vavezhdam*

insomnia безсъние *bezsanye*

instant message незабавно съобщение *nezabavno saobshtenye*

insulin инсулин *insulin*

insurance застраховка *zastrahovka*; **~ card** здравноосигурителна карта *zdravno-osiguritelna karta*; **~ company** застрахователна фирма *zastrahovatelna firma*

interesting интересен *interesen*

intermediate междинен *mezhdinen*, среден *sreden*

international международен *mezhdunaroden*; **~ flight**

международен полет *mezhdunaroden polet*; **~ student card** международна студентска карта *mezhdunarodna studentska karta*

internet интернет *internet*; **~ cafe** интернет кафе *internet kafe*; **~ service** интернет услуги *internet uslugi*

interpreter преводач *prevodach*

intersection кръстовище *krastovishte*

intestine черво *chervo*

introduce *v* (person) представям *predstavyam*

invoice *n* [BE] сметка *smetka*, фактура *faktura*

Ireland Ирландия *irlandiya*

Irish *adj* ирландски *irlandski*

iron *v* гладя *gladya*; **~ n** (clothes) ютия *youtiya*

Italian *adj* италиански *italyanski*

J

jacket *n* яке *yake*, сако *sako*

Japanese *adj* японски *yaponski*

jar *n* (for jam etc) буркан *burkan*

jaw *n* челюст *chelyoust*

jazz *n* джаз *dzhaz*; **~ club** джаз клуб *dzhaz klub*

jeans дънки *danki*

jet ski *n* джет ски *dzhet ski*

jeweler бижутер *bizhuter*, златар *zlatar*

jewelry бижутерия *bizhuteriya*

join *v* (go with somebody) съпровождам *saprovozhdam*, идвам с *idvam s*

joint *n* (body part) става *stava*

K

key *n* ключ *klyouch*; **~ card** ключ карта *klyouch karta*, **~ring** ключодържател *klyouchodarzhatel*

kiddie pool детски басейн *detski baseyn*

kidney (body part) бъбрек *babrek*

kilo кило *kilo*; **~gram** килограм *kilogram*; **~meter** километър *kilometar*

kiss *v* целувам *tseluvam*

kitchen кухня *kuhnya*; **~ foil** [BE] кухненско фолио *kuhnensko folyo*

knee *n* коляно *kolyano*

knife *n* нож *nozh*

kosher *adj* кашерен *kasheren*

L

lace *n* (fabric) дантела *dantela decorative cloth*, връзка за обувка *vrazka za obuvki* (for shoes)

lactose intolerant непоносимост към лактоза *neponosimot kam laktoza*

lake езеро *ezero*

large голям *golyam*

last *adj* последен *posleden*

late (time) късно *kasno*

launderette [BE] пералня на самообслужване *peralnya na samo:bsluzhvane*

laundromat пералня на самообслужване *peralnya na samo:bsluzhvane*

laundry (place) пералня *peralnya* **~ service** услуги пране на дрехи *uslugi prane na drehi*

lawyer *n* юрист *yourist*, адвокат *advokat*

leather *n* кожа *kozha*

leave *v* (hotel) напускам *napuskam*; **~ (plane)** излитам *izlitam*

left *adj, adv* (direction) наляво *nalyavo*

leg *n* крак *krak*

lens лещи *leshti*

less по-малко *po-malko*

lesson *n* урок *urok*; **take ~s** вземам уроци *vzemam urotsi*

letter *n* писмо *pismo*

library библиотека *biblyoteka*

life jacket спасителна жилетка *spasitelna zhiletka*

lifeguard спасител *spasitel*

lift *n* [BE] лифт *lift*; **~ n** (ride) качване с лифт *kachvane s lift*; **~ pass** лифт карта *lift karta*

light *n* (cigarette) лайт
layt~ n (overhead)
осветление *osvetlenye*;
~bulb крушка
krushka

lighter *n* запалка *zapalka*

like *v* харесвам
haresvam

line *n* (train/bus)
линия *liniya*

linen спално бельо
spalno belyo (in
the bed), лен *len*
(material)

lip *n* устна *ustna*

liquor store магазин
с алкохол *magazin s
alkohol*

liter литър *litar*

little малко *malko*

live *v* живея *zhiveya*;
~ music музика на
живо *muzika na zhivo*

liver (body part) черен
дроб *cheren drob*

loafers мокасини
mokasini

local *n* (person)
местен *mesten*

lock *v* заключвам
zaklyouchvam ~ n
ключалка *klyouchalka*

locker шкафче *shkafche*

log off *v* (computer)
излизам *izlizam*

log on *v* (computer)
логвам се *logvam se*

long *adj* дълъг
dalag; **~-sighted** [BE]
далекоглед *dalekogled*;
~-sleeved с дълъг
ръкав *s dalag rakav*

look *v* гледам *gledam*;
~ for something
търся *tarsya*

loose (fit) свободен
svoboden

lose *v* (something)
губя *gubya*

lost изгубен *izguben*;
~-and-found бюро за
изгубени/намерени
вещи *byouro za
izgubeni/namereni veshti*

lotion лосион *losyon*

louder по-силно
po silno

love *v* (someone)
обичам *obicham*; **~ n**
любов *lyoubov*

low *adj* нисък *nisak*

luggage багаж *bagazh*;
~ cart количка за
багаж *kolichka za
bagazh*; **~ locker**
багажен шкаф *baga-
zhen shkav*; **~ ticket**
багажен етикет
bagazhen etiket

lunch *n* обяд *obyad*

lung бял дроб *byal drob*

luxury car луксозна
кола *luksozna kola*

M

machine washable за
пране в пералня *za
prane v peralnya*

magazine списание
spisanye

magnificent
великолепен
velikolepen

mail *v* изпращам
izprashtam; **~ n** ; **~box**
пощенска кутия
poshtenska kutiya

main attraction
основна атракция
osnovna atraktsiya

main course основно
ястие *osnovno yastie*

mall мол *mol*

man (adult male) мъж
mazh

manager управител
upravitel, мениджър
menidzhar

manicure *n* маникюр
manikyour

manual car кола с
ръчна скоростна
кутия *kola s rachna
skorostna kutiya*

map *n* карта *karta*;
~ n (town) карта на
града *karta na grada*

market *n* пазар *pazar*

married женен *zhenen*

marry женя се
zhenya se

mass *n* (church
service) литургия
liturgiya

massage *n* масаж
masazh

match *n* среща *sreshta*
(sport game), кибрит
kibrit (to start fire)

meal ядене *yadene*

measure *v* (someone)
оценявам *otsenyavam*

measuring cup
мерителна чаша
meritelna chasha

measuring spoon
мерителна лъжица
meritelna lazhitsa

mechanic *n* механик
mehanik

medication (drugs)
медикамент *medika-
ment*, лекарство
lekarstvo

medicine медицина
meditsina, лекарство
lekarstvo

medium (steak)
средно изпържен
sredno izparzhen

meet *v* срещам
sreshtam

meeting *n* (business)
среща *sreshta*;
~ room конферентна
зала *konferentna zala*

membership card
членска карта
chlenska karta

memorial (place)
паметник *pametnik*

memory card карта
памет *karta pamet*

mend *v* (clothes)
закърпвам *zakarpvam*

menstrual cramps
менструални болки
mrnstrualni bolki

menu (restaurant)
меню *menyou*

message съобщение
saobshtenye

meter *n* (parking) брояч
broyach; **~ n** (measure)
метър *metar*

microwave *n*
микровълнова печка
mikrovalnova pechka

midday [BE] обед *obed*

midnight полунощ
polunosht

mileage пробег *probeg*

mini-bar мини-бар
mini bar

minute минута *minuta*

missing (not there)
отсъстващ *otsastvasht*
(person), липсващ
lipsvasht (person or
object)

mistake *n* грешка
greshka

mobile home каравана
karavana

mobile phone [BE]
мобилен телефон
mobilen telefon

mobility мобилност
mobilnost

monastery манастир
manastir

money пари *pari*

month месец *mesets*

mop *n* моп *mop*

moped мотопед *motoped*

more повече *poveche*

morning *n* сутрин *sutrin*

mosque джамия *dzhamiya*

mother *n* майка *mayka*

motion sickness морска
болест *morska bolest*,
кинетоза *kinetoza*

motor *n* двигател *dviga-
tel*; **~ boat** моторна
лодка *motorna lodka*;
~cycle мотоциклет
mototsiklet; **~way**
[BE] автомагистрала
avtomagistrala

mountain планина
planina; **~ bike**
планински велосипед
planinski velosiped

mousse (hair) пяна за
коса *pyana za kosa*

mouth *n* уста *usta*

movie *n* филм *film*; **~**
theater киносалон
kinosalon

mug *v* чаша *chasha*

multiple-trip ticket
билет за многократно
пътуване *bilet za
mnogokratno patuvane*

muscle *n* мускул *muskul*

museum музей *muzey*

music музика *muzika*;
~ store музикален
магазин *muzikalen
magazin*

N

nail file пила за нокти
pila za nokti

nail salon салон за
маникюр *salon za
manikyour*

name *n* име *ime*

napkin салфетка
salfetka

nappy [BE] пелена
pelena

nationality народност
narodnost

nature preserve
природен резерват
priroden rezervat

nausea гадене *gadene*

nauseous отвратителен
otvratitelen

near близо *blizo*;
~-sighted късоглед
kasogled

nearby наблизо *nablizo*

neck *n* врат *vrat*, шия
shiya

necklace огърлица
ogarlitsa

need *v* нуждая се
nuzhdaya se

newspaper вестник
vestnik

newsstand павилион
за вестници *pavilion
za vestnitsi*

next *adj* следващ
sledvasht

nice приятен *priyaten*

night нощ *nosht*; **~club**
нощен клуб *noshten
klub*

no не *ne*; **~ (not any)**
никакъв *nikakav*

non-alcoholic
безалкохолен
bezalkoholen

non-smoking *adj*

за непушачи *za
nepushachi*

noon *n* обед *obed*

north *n* север *sever*

nose нос *nos*

note *n* **[BE] (money)**
банкнота *banknota*

nothing нищо *nishto*

notify *v* съобщавам
saobshtavam

novice начинаещ
nachinaesht

now сега *sega*

number *n* номер *nomer*

nurse *n* медицинска
сестра *meditsinska
sestra*

O

office бюро *byouro*;
~ hours работно
време *rabotno vreme*

off-licence [BE]
магазин с алкохол
magazin s alkohol

oil *n* олио *olyo*

OK добре *dobre*

old *adj* стар *star*

on the corner на ъгъла
na agala

once (one time)
веднъж *vednazh*

one (counting)
един *edin*; **~-day**
(ticket) еднодневен
билет *ednodneven
bilet*; **~-way ticket**
(airline) еднопосочен
самолетен билет *ed-
noposochen samoleten
bilet*; **(bus/train/**
subway) еднопосочен
билет *ednoposochen
bilet*; **~-way street**
еднопосочна улица
ednoposochna ulitsa

only само *samo*

open *v* отварям *ot-
varyam*; **~** *adj* отворен
otvoren

opera опера *opera*;
~ house опера *opera*

opposite *n*
противоположност *proti-
vopolozhnost* (noun sth
absolutely opposite),
срещу *sreshtu*(prep. =
in front of)

optician оптик *optik*

orange *adj* **(color)**
оранжев *oranzhev*

orchestra оркестър
orkestar

order *v* **(restaurant)**
поръчвам *porachvam*

outdoor pool открит
басейн *otkrit baseyn*

outside *prep* навън
navan

over *prep* **(direction)**
над *nad*; **~done**
(meat) препечен
prepechen; **~heat** *v*
(car) прегрян *pre-
gryan*; **~look** *n* **(scenic**
place) гледка *gledka*;
~night през нощта
prez noshta; **~-the-**
counter (medication)
продаван без рецепта
prodavan bez retsepta

oxygen treatment
кислородна терапия
kislorodna terapiya

P

pm след обед *sled obed*

pacifier биберон
biberon

pack *v* опаковам
opakovam

package *n* пакет *paket*

pad *n* [BE] превръзка *prevrazka* (for ladies), кърпичка *karpichka* (to wipe sth.)

paddling pool [BE] детски басейн *detski baseyn*

pain болка *bolka*

pajamas пижама *pizhama*

palace дворец *dvorets*

pants панталон *pantalon*

pantyhose чорапогащи *chorapogashti*

paper *n* (material) хартия *hartiya*; ~ **towel** хартиена кърпа *hartiyena karpa*

paracetamol [BE] парацетамол *paratsetamol*

park *v* паркирам *parkiram*; ~ *n* парк; ~**ing garage** гараж за паркиране *garazh za parkirane*; ~**ing lot** паркинг *parking*; ~**ing meter** паркинг автомат *parking avtomat*

parliament building сграда на народно събрание *sgrada na narodno sabranie*

part (for car) част *chast*; ~**-time** *adj* на частично време *na chastichno vreme*

pass through *v* (travel) минавам през *minavam prez*

passenger пътник *patnik*

passport паспорт *pasport*; ~ **control** паспортен контрол

пасporten контрол

password парола *parola*

pastry shop сладкарница *sladkarnitsa*

patch *v* (clothing) закърпвам *zakarpvam*

path път *pat*

pay *v* плащам *plashtam*; ~**phone** уличен телефон *ulichen telefon*

peak *n* (of a mountain) връх *vrah*

pearl перла *perla*

pedestrian *n* пешеходец *peshehodets*

pediatrician педиатър *pedyatar*

pedicure *n* педикюр *pedikyour*

pen *n* химикал *himikal*

penicillin пеницилин *penitsilin*

penis пенис *penis*

per на *na*; ~ **day** на ден *na den*; ~ **hour** на час *na chas*; ~ **night** на нощ *na nosht*; ~ **week** на седмица *na sedmitsa*

perfume *n* парфюм *parfyoum*

period (menstrual) менструация *menstruatsiya*; ~ (of time) период *period*

permit *v* разрешавам *razreshavam*

petrol [BE] бензин *benzin*; ~ **station** [BE] бензиностанция *benzinostantsiya*

pewter пютър *pyoutar*, калай *kalay*

pharmacy аптека *apteka*

phone *v* позвънявам *pozvanyavam*; ~ *n* телефон *telefon*; ~ **call** телефонно обаждане *telefonno obazhdane*; ~ **card** телефонна карта *telefonna karta*; ~ **number** телефонен номер *telefonen nomer*

photo снимка *snimka*; ~**copy** ксерокопие *kserokopie*; ~**graphy** фотография *fotografiya*

pick up *v* (person) вземам *vzemam*

picnic area място за пикник *myasto za piknik*

piece *n* парче *parche*

Pill (birth control) таблетка *tabletka* (for birth control => антиконцепционна таблетка *antikontseptsyonna tabletka*)

pillow *n* възглавница *vazglavnitsa*

pink *adj* розов *rozov*

piste [BE] ски писта *ski pista*; ~ **map** [BE] карта на писти *karta na pisti*

pizzeria пицария *pitsariya*

place *v* (a bet) залагам *zalagam*

plane *n* самолет *samolet*

plastic wrap фолио *folyo*

plate *n* чиния *chiniya* (dish), блюдо *blyoudo*

platform [BE] (train) перон *peron*

platinum *n* платина *platina*

play *v* играя *igraya*; ~ *n* (theatre) пиеса *piesa*; ~**ground** игрище *igrishte*; ~**pen** кошарка за деца *kosharka za detsa*

please *adv* моля *molya* (verb), pleased – доволен *dovolen*

pleasure *n* удоволствие *udovolstve*

plunger плунжер *plunzher*

plus size голям размер *golyam razmer*

pocket *n* джоб *dzhob*

poison *n* отрова *otrova*

poles (skiing) щеки *shteki*

police полиция *politsiya*; ~ **report** полицейски доклад *politseyski doklad*; ~ **station** полицейски участък *politseyski uchastak*

pond *n* езерце *ezertse*

pool *n* басейн *baseyn*

pop music поп музика *pop muzika*

portion *n* порция *portsiya*

post *n* [BE] поща *poshta*; ~ **office** поща *poshta*; ~**box** [BE] пощенска кутия *poshtenska kutiya*; ~**card** пощенска картичка *poshtenska kartichka*

pot *n* тенджера *tendzhera*

pottery керамика *keramika*

pound n (weight) фунт funt; **~** (British sterling) британска лира britanska lira

pregnant бременна bremenna

prescribe (medication) предписвам predpisvam

prescription рецепта retsepta

press v (clothing) гладя gladya

price n цена tsena

print v разпечатвам razpechatvam; **~** n разпечатка razpechatka

problem проблем problem

produce n плодове и зеленчуци plodove i zelenchutsi (in sense of fruits and vegetables) **~ store** магазин за плодове и зеленчуци magazin za plodove i zelenchutsi

prohibit забранявам zabranyavam

pronounce произнасям proiznasyam

Protestant протестант protestant

public adj обществен obshtestven

pull v тегля teglya

purple adj виолетов vyoletov, пурпурен purpuren

purse n портмоне portmone

push v бутам butam; **~chair** [BE] детска количка detska kolichka

quality n качество kachestvo

question n въпрос vapros

quiet adj тих tih, спокоен spokoen

R

racetrack писта pista

racket n (sports) ракета raketa

railway station [BE] железопътна гара zhelezopatna gara

rain n дъжд dazhd; **~coat** дъждобран dazhdobran; **~forest** тропическа гора tropicheska gora; **~y** дъждовен dazhdoven

rap n (music) рап rap

rape v изнасилвам iznasilvam; **~** n изнасилване iznasilvane

rare рядък ryadak (not often - e.g. rare case), много малко изпържен mnogo malko izparzhen (for steaks)

rash n обрив obriv

ravine дефиле defile

razor blade ножче за бръснене nozhche za brasnene

reach v постигам postigam

ready готов gotov

real adj действителен deystvitelen

receipt n касова бележка kasova belezhka, квитанция kvitantsiya

receive v получавам poluchavam

reception (hotel) рецепция (retseptsiya)

recharge v зареждам zarezhdam

recommend препоръчвам preporachvam

recommendation препоръка preporaka

recycling рециклиране retsiklirane

red adj червен cherven

refrigerator хладилник hladilnik

region регион regyon

registered mail препоръчано писмо preporachano pismo

regular n (fuel) обикновено гориво obiknoveno gorivo

relationship връзка vrazka

rent v наемам naemam; **~** n наем naem

rental car кола под наем kola pod naem

repair v ремонтирам remontiram

repeat v повтарям povtaryam

reservation резервация rezervatsiya; **~ desk** бюро за резервации byouro za rezervatsi

reserve v (hotel) резервирам rezerviram, правя резервация pravia rezervatsiya

restaurant ресторант restorant

restroom тоалетна toaletna

retired adj (from work) пенсиониран

pensioniran

return v (something) връщам vrashtam; **~** n [BE] (trip) връщане vrashtane

reverse v (the charges of a phone call) [BE] звъня за сметка на приемащия zvanya za smetka na priyemashtya (verb = to make a call with the receiving person paying)

rib n (body part) ребро rebro

right adj, adv (direction) десен desen; надясна nadyasno; **~ of way** предимство predimstvo

ring n пръстен prasten

river река reka

road map пътна карта patna karta

rob v ограбвам ograbvam, обирам obiram

robbed ограбен ograben

romantic adj романтичен romantichen

room n стая staya; **~ key** ключ за стая klyouch za staya; **~ service** румсървиз rumserviz

round trip отиване и връщане otivane i vrashtane

route n път pat

rowboat гребна лодка grebna lodka

rubbing alcohol медицински спирт meditsinski spirt

rubbish n [BE] боклук bokluk; **~ bag** [BE] торба за боклук torba za bokluk

S

rugby n ръгби *ragbi*

ruin n развалини *razvalini*

rush n бързане *barzane*

sad adj тъжен *tazhen*

safe adj (protected) безопасен *bezopasen*; ~ n (thing) сейф *seyf*

sales tax данък продажба *danak prodazhba*

same adj същ *sasht*

sandals сандали *sandali*

sanitary napkin дамска превръзка *damska prevrazka*

sauna сауна *sauna*

sauté v пека *peka*

save v (computer) записвам *zapisvam*

savings (account) спестявния *spestya-vaniya*

scanner скенер *skener*

scarf шал *shal*

schedule v планирам *planiram*; ~ n програма *programa*

school n училище *uchilishte*

science наука *nauka*

scissors ножица *nozhitsa*

sea море *more*

seat n седалка *sedalka*

security охрана *ohrana*

see v виждам *vizhdam*

self-service n самообслужване *samo:bsluzhvane*

sell v продавам *prodavam*

seminar семинар *seminar*

send v изпращам *izprashtam*

senior citizen пенсионер *pensyoner*

separated (person) разделен *razdelen*

serious сериозен *seryozen*

service (in a restaurant) обслужване *obsluzhvane*

sexually transmitted disease (STD) болести, предавани по полов път *bolesti predavani po polov pat*

shampoo n шампоан *shampoan*

sharp adj остър *ostar*

shaving cream крем за бръснене *krem za brasnene*

sheet n (bed) одеяло *odeyalo*

ship v изпращам *izprashtam*

shirt блуза *bluza*, риза *riza*

shoe store магазин за обувки *magazin za obuvki*

shoe обувка *obuvka*

shop v купувам *kupuvam*; ~ n магазин *magazin*

shopping n пазаруване *pazaruvane*; ~ area търговска зона *targovska zona*; ~ centre [BE] търговски център *targovski tsentar*; ~ mall мол *mol*

short къс *kas*; ~-sleeved с къс ръкав *s kas rakav*

shorts къси панталони *kasi pantaloni*

short-sighted [BE] късоглед *kasogled*

shoulder n рамо *ramo*

show v показвам *pokazvam*

shower n (bath) душ *dush*

shrine светилище *svetilishte*

sick adj болен *bolen*

side n страна *strana*; ~ dish гарнитура *garnitura*; ~ effect страничен ефект *stranichen efekt*; ~ order гарнитура *garnitura*

sightseeing разглеждане на забележителностите *razglezhdane na zabelezhitelnosti*; ~ tour туристическа обиколка *turisticheska obikolka*

sign n (document) подписвам *podpisvam*

silk коприна *koprina*

silver n сребро *srebro*

single adj (person) сингъл *singal*; ~ bed единично легло *edinichno leglo*; ~ print едно копие *edno kopye*; ~ room единична стая *edinichna staya*

sink n мивка *mivka*

sister n сестра *sestra*

sit v сядам *syadam*, седя *sedya*

size n размер *razmer*

ski v карам ски *karam ski*; ~ n ски *ski*; ~ lift лифт *lift*

skin n кожа *kozha*

skirt n пола *pola*

sleep v спя *spya*; ~er car бърза кола *barza kola*; ~ing bag спален чувал *spalen chuval*; ~ing car [BE] спален вагон *spalen vagon*

slice n парче *parche* (piece of sth), резен *rezen*

slippers чехли *chehli*

slower по-бавно по *bavno*

slowly бавно *bavno*

small малък *malak*

smoke v пуша *pusha*

smoking (area) зона за пушачи *zona za pushachi*

snack bar снекбар *snekbar*

sneakers гуменки *gumenki*

snowboard n сноуборд *snoubord*

snowshoe n снегоходки *snegohodki*

snowy снежен *snezhen*

soap n сапун *sapun*

soccer футбол *futbol*

sock чорап *chorap*

some (with singular nouns) малко *malko*; ~ (with plural nouns) някои *niakoi* (some people), няколко *nyakolko*

soother [BE] биберон *biberon*

sore throat болка на гърло *bolka na garlo*

south n юг *youg*

souvenir n сувенир *suvenir*; ~ store сувенирен магазин *suveniren magazin*

spa спа *spa*

spatula шпатула *shpatula*

speak v говоря *govorya*

specialist (doctor) специалист *spetsialist*

specimen мостра *mostra*, екземпляр *egzemplyar*

speeding превишаване на скорост *previshavane na skorost*

spell v изговарям дума буква по буква *izgovaryam duma bukva po bukva*

spicy лютив *lyutiv*; ~ **(not bland)** груб *grub*

spine (body part) гръбнак *grabnak*

spoon n лъжица *lazhitsa*

sport спорт *sport*; ~ **massage** спортен масаж *sporten masazh*

sprain n навяхване *navyahvane*

stadium стадион *stadyon*

stairs стълби *stalbi*

stamp v **(ticket)** таксувам *taksuvam*; ~ n **(postage)** пощенска марка *poshtenska marka*

start v започвам *zapochvam*

starter [BE] предястие *predyastye*, стартер *starter*

station n **(stop)** гара *gara*; **bus** ~ автогара *avtogara*; **gas** ~ бензиностант-

siya; **petrol** ~ **[BE]** бензиностанция *benzinostantsiya*;

subway ~ станция на метро *stantsiya na metro*; **train** ~ ЖП гара *zhe pe gara*

statue статуя *statuya*

steakhouse ресторант за бифтеци *restorant za biftetsi*

steal v крада *krada*

steep adj стръмен *stramen*

sterling silver стерлингово сребро *sterlingovo srebro*

sting n ужилване *uzhilvane*, жило *zhilo*

stolen краден *kraden*

stomach корем *korem*; ~**ache** коремна болка *koremna bolka*

stool (bowel movement) изпражнения *izprazhneniya*

stop v **(bus)** спирам *spiram*; ~ n **(transportation)** спирка *spirka*

store directory (mall) списък на магазини *spisak na magazini*

storey [BE] етаж *etazh*

stove n печка *pechka*

straight adv **(direction)** направо *napravo*

strange странен *stranen*

stream n поток *potok*

stroller (baby) детска количка *detska kolichka*

student (university) студент *student*;

~ **(school)** ученик *uchenik*

study v следвам *sledvam*; ~**ing** n изучаване *izuchavane*

stuffed пълнен *palnen* (sing), пълнени *palneni* (pl)

stunning зашеметяващ *zashemetyavasht*, красив *krasiv*

subtitle n субтитри *subtitri* > ~ **station** подстанция *podstantsiya*

suit n костюм *kostyoum*; ~**case** куфар *kufar*

sun n слънце *slantse*; ~**block** слънцезащитен крем *slantsezashtiten krem*; ~**burn** слънчево изгаряне *slanchevo izgaryane*; ~**glasses** слънчеви очила *slanchevi ochila*; ~**ny** слънчев *slanchev*; ~**screen** слънцезащитен крем *slantsezashtiten krem*; ~**stroke** слънчев удар *slanchev udar*

super n **(fuel)** супер гориво *super gorivo*; ~**market** супермаркет *supermarket*

surfboard сърф *sarf*

surgical spirit [BE] медицински спирт *meditsinski spirt*

swallow v гълтам *galtam*

sweater пуловер *pulover*

sweachirt спортна блуза *sportna bluza*

sweet n **[BE]** любим *lyoubim* (masc), любима *lyoubima* (fem); ~ adj **(taste)** сладък *sladak*

swelling подутина *podutina*

swim v плувам *pluvam*; ~**suit** бански костюм *banski kostyoum*

symbol (keyboard) символ *simvol*

synagogue синагога *sinagoga*

T

table n маса *masa*

tablet (medicine) таблетка *tabletka*

take v взeмам *vzemam*

tampon n тампон *tampon*

taste v **(test)** пробвам *probvam*

taxi n такси *taksi*

team n екип *ekip*

teaspoon чаена лъжичка *chaena lazhichka*

telephone n телефон *telefon*

temple (religious) църква *tsarkva*

temporary временен *vremenen*

tennis тенис *tenis*

tent n палатка *palatka*; ~ **peg** колче за палатка *kolche za palatka*; ~ **pole** рейка за палатка *reyka za palatka*

terminal n **(airport)** терминал *terminal*

terrible ужасен *uzhasen*

text v **(send a message)** изпращам sms съобщение *izprashtam esemes saobshtenye*; **~** n sms съобщение *esemes saobshtenye*

thank v благодаря *blagodarya*; **~ you** благодаря ти *blagodarya ti*

theater театър *teatar*

theft кражба *krazhba*

there там *tam*

thief крадец *kradets*

thigh бедро *bedro*

thirsty жаден *zhaden*

this този *tozi* [masc.], тази *tazi* [fem.], това *tova* [neutr.]

throat гърло *garlo*

thunderstorm гръмотевична буря *gramotevichna burya*

ticket n билет *bilet*; **~ office** билетно бюро *biletno byouro*

tie n **(clothing)** вратовръзка *vratovrazka*

tight (fit) плътно прилягащ *platno prilyagasht*

tights чорапогащи *chorapogashti*

time време *vreme*; **~table** [BE] **(transportation)** разписание *razpisanye*

tire n гума *guma*

tired изморен *izmoren*

tissue кърпичка *karpichka*

tobacconist магазин с цигари *magazin s tsigari*

today adv днес *dnes*

toe n пръст на крака *prast na kraka*

toenail нокът на крака *nokat na kraka*

toilet [BE] тоалетна *toaletna*; **~ paper** тоалетна хартия *toaletna hartiya*

tomorrow adv утре *utre*

tongue n език *ezik*

tonight довечера *dovechera*

tooth зъб *zab*

toothpaste паста за зъби *pasta za zabi*

total n **(amount)** общо *obshto*

tough adj **(food)** жилав *zhilav*

tour n обиколка *obikolka*

tourist турист *turist*; **~ information office** туристическа информация *turisticheska informatsiya*

tow truck пътна помощ *patna pomosht*

towel n кърпа *karpa*

tower n кула *kula*

town град *grad*; **~ hall** кметство *kmetstvo*; **~ map** карта на града *karta na grada*; **~ square** площада *ploshtad*

toy играчка *igrachka*; **~ store** магазин за играчки *magazin za igrachki*

track n **(train)** железопътна линия *zhelezopatna liniya*

traditional традиционен

traditsyonen

traffic light светофар *svetofar*

trail n (ski) ски писта *ski pista*; **~** map карта на ски писти *karta na ski pisti*

trailer (car) каравана *karavana*

train n влак *vlak*; **~ station** ЖП гара *zhe pe gara*

transfer v **(change trains/flights)** прекачвам се *prekachvam se*; **~ (money)** превеждам пари *prevezhdam pari*

translate превеждам *prevezhdam*

trash n боклук *bokluk*

travel n пътуване *patuvane*; **~ agency** туристическа агенция *turisticheska agentsiya*; **~ sickness** морска болест *morska bolest*; **~ers check [cheque BE]** пътнически чек *patnicheski chek*

tree дърво *darvo*

trim (hair) v подстригвам *podstrigvam*

trip n пътешествие *pateshestvie*, пътуване *patuvane*

trolley [BE] **(grocery store)** количка *kolichka*; **~** [BE] **(luggage)** количка за багаж *kolichka za bagazh*

trousers [BE] панталон *pantalon*

T-shirt тениска *teniska*

tumble dry центрофугиране *tsentrofugirane*

turn off v **(device)** изключвам *izklyouchvam*

turn on v **(device)** включвам *vklyouchvam*

TV телевизия *televiziya*

tyre [BE] гума *guma*

U

ugly грозен *grozen*

umbrella чадър *chadar*

unbranded medication [BE] немаркови лекарства *nemarkovi lekarstva*

unconscious (faint) без съзнание *bez saznanye*

underdone недопечен *nedopechen*

underground n [BE] метро *metro*; **~ station** [BE] станция на метро *stantsiya na metro*

underpants [BE] гащи *gashti*

understand v разбирам *razbiram*

underwear бельо *belyo*

United Kingdom (UK) Великобритания *velikobritaniya*

United States (US) Съединените Щати *saedinenite shtati*

university университет *universitet*

unleaded (gas) безоловен *bezoloven*

upset stomach стомашно разстройство *stomashno razstroystvo*

urgent спешен *speshen*
urine урина *urina*
use v използвам *izpolzvam*
username потребителско име *potrebitelsko ime*
utensil прибор *pribor*

V

vacancy (room) свободна стая (vacant room) *svobodna staya*
vacation n отпуск *otpusk*
vaccination ваксинация *vaksinatsiya*
vacuum cleaner прахосмукачка *prahosmukachka*
vaginal infection вагинална инфекция *vaginalna infektsiya*
valid валиден *validen*
valley долина *dolina*
valuable adj ценен *tsenen*
value n стойност *stoynost*
van ван *van*
VAT [BE] ДДС *de de se*
vegan n веган *vegan*; ~ adj вегански *veganski*
vegetarian n вегетарианец *vegetaryanets* (he), вегетарианка *vegetaryanka* (she); ~ adj вегетариански *vegetaryanski*
vehicle registration регистрационен номер *registratsyonen nomer*
viewpoint (scenic)

[BE] място с красива гледка *myasto s krasiva gledka*
village село *selo*
vineyard лозе *loze* **(place where grapes grow)**, винарна *vinarna* **(place where you can buy/drink wine)**
visa виза *viza*
visit v посещавам *poseshtavam*; ~ing hours приемни часове *priyemni chasove*
visually impaired с увредено зрение *s uvredeno zrenye*
vitamin витамин *vitamin*
V-neck шпиц деколте *shpits dekolte*
volleyball game волейболен мач *voleybolen mach*
vomit v повръщам *povrashtam*; ~ing повръщане *povrashtane*

W

wait v чакам *chakam*; ~ n изчакване *izchakvane*
waiter сервитьор *servityor*
waiting room чакалня *chakalnya*
waitress сервитьорка *servityorka*
wake v събуждам *sabuzhdam* (somebody), събуждам се *sabuzhdam se* (myself); ~up call събуждане по телефона *sabuzhdane po telefona*

walk v ходя *hodya*; ~ n ~ing route пешеходна пътека *peshehodna pateka*
wallet портфейл *portfeyl*
war memorial военен паметник *voenen pametnik*
warm v (something) топля *toplya*; ~ adj (temperature) топъл *topal*
washing machine перална *peralnya*
watch v гледам *gledam*
waterfall водопад *vodopad*
wax v (hair) нанасям восък за коса *nanasyam vosak za kosa*
weather n време *vreme*
week седмица *sedmitsa*; ~end уикенд *uikend*
weekly седмично *sedmichno*
welcome adj добре дошли *dobre doshli*; **you're** ~ няма защо *nyama zashto*, заповядайте *zapovyadayte*
west n запад *zapad*
what какво *kakvo*
wheelchair инвалидна количка *invalidna kolichka*; ~ **ramp** рампа за инвалидна количка *rampa za invalidna kolichka*
when adv (at what time) кога *koga*
where къде *kade*
white adj бял *byal*; ~ **gold** бяло злато

byalo zlato
who (question) кой *koy*
widowed овдовял *ovdovyal*
wife съпруга *sapruga*
window прозорец *prozorets*; ~ **case** калъф *kalav*
wine list меню с вина *menyou s vina*
wireless безжичен *bezzhichen*; ~ **phone** безжичен телефон *bezzhichen telefon* (mobile phone = мобилен телефон *mobilen telefon*)
with с *s*
withdraw v (money) тегля *teglya*; ~**al** (bank) теглене на пари *teglene na pari*
without без *bez*
woman жена *zhena*
wool вълна *valna*
work v работя *rabotya*
wrap v опаковам *opakovam*
wrist китка *kitka*
write v пиша *pisha*

Y

year година *godina*
yellow adj жълт *zhalt*
yes да *da*
yesterday adv вчера *vchera*
young adj млад *mlad*
youth hostel младежко общежитие *mladezhko obshtezhitye*

Z

zoo зоологическа градина *zo:logicheska gradina*

INDEX

BULGARIA

Fourth Edition 2018

Editor: Rachel Lawrence
Author: Craig Turp
Head of Production: Rebeka Davies
Picture Editor: Tom Smyth
Cartography Update: Carte
Update Production: Apa Digital
Photography Credits: Alamy 43, 106;
Balkanpix.com/REX/Shutterstock 5M, 38;
FLPA/REX/Shutterstock 86; Getty Images
1, 4MC, 22, 26, 41, 61, 82, 89, 102; iStock
4TC, 4ML, 4TL, 5T, 5TC, 5MC, 5M, 6L, 11,
13, 14, 28, 30, 33, 34, 37, 47, 51, 56, 62, 64,
65, 68, 72, 81, 84, 91, 93; Patrick Frilet/REX/
Shutterstock 20; Shutterstock 5MC, 6R, 7,
19, 44, 46, 48, 53, 54, 58, 59, 67, 71, 74, 77,
78, 94, 97, 99, 101, 105; Starwood Hotles &
Resorts 7R; SuperStock 17
Cover Picture: iStock

Distribution
UK, Ireland and Europe: Apa Publications
(UK) Ltd; sales@insightguides.com
United States and Canada: Ingram
Publisher Services; ips@ingramcontent.com
Australia and New Zealand: Woodslane;
info@woodslane.com.au
Southeast Asia: Apa Publications (SN) Pte;
singaporeoffice@insightguides.com
Worldwide: Apa Publications (UK) Ltd;
sales@insightguides.com

**Special Sales, Content Licensing
and CoPublishing**
Insight Guides can be purchased in bulk
quantities at discounted prices. We can
create special editions, personalised jackets
and corporate imprints tailored to your
needs. sales@insightguides.com;
www.insightguides.biz

Contact us
Every effort has been made to provide
accurate information in this publication,
but changes are inevitable. The publisher
cannot be responsible for any resulting loss,
inconvenience or injury. We would appreciate
it if readers would call our attention to any
errors or outdated information. We also
welcome your suggestions; please contact
us at: berlitz@apaguide.co.uk
www.insightguides.com/berlitz

Berlitz Trademark Reg. U.S. Patent Office
and other countries. Marca Registrada.
Used under licence from the Berlitz
Investment Corporation

Berlitz®

speaking your language

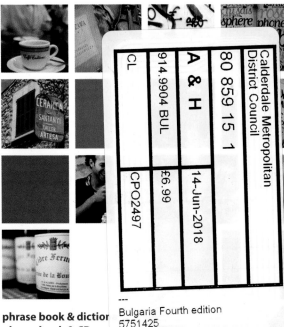

phrase book & diction...
phrase book & CD

Available in: Arabic, Brazilian Portuguese*, Burmese*, Cantonese
Chinese, Croatian, Czech*, Danish*, Dutch, English, Filipino, Finnish*, French,
German, Greek, Hebrew*, Hindi*, Hungarian*, Indonesian, Italian, Japanese,
Korean, Latin American Spanish, Malay, Mandarin Chinese, Mexican Spanish,
Norwegian, Polish, Portuguese, Romanian*, Russian, Spanish, Swedish, Thai,
Turkish, Vietnamese
*Book only

www.berlitzpublishing.com